The Path
to
Bodhidharma

The Path to Bodhidharma

The Teachings of Shodo Harada Roshi

Translated by *Priscilla Daichi Storandt*
Edited by *Jane Lago*

TUTTLE PUBLISHING
BOSTON · RUTLAND, VERMONT · TOKYO

First published in 2000 by Tuttle Publishing, an imprint of Periplus Editions (HK) Ltd, with editorial offices at 153 Milk Street, Boston, Massachusetts 02109.

Copyright © 2000 by One Drop Zendo Association

All rights reserved. No part of this publication may be reproduced or utilized in any form or by any means, electronic or mechanical, including photocopying, recording, or by any information storage and retrieval system, without prior written permission from Tuttle Publishing.

Library of Congress Cataloging-in-Publication Data
Harada, Shodo.
   The path to Bodhidharma : the teachings of Shodo Harada Roshi / edited by Jane Lago ; translated by Pricilla Storandt ; calligraphy by Shodo Harada.
     p. cm.
   Original title not available. Cf. CIP data sheet
   ISBN 0-8048-3216-1 (pbk.)
   1. Spiritual life--Zen Buddhism. 2. Spiritual life--Rinzai (Sect) 3. Zen Buddhism--doctrines. I. Lago, Jane. II. Title.
BQ9288 .H35 2000
294.3'4--dc21   00-027769

Distributed by

USA
Tuttle Publishing
Distribution Center
Airport Industrial Park
364 Innovation Drive
North Clarendon, VT 05759-9436
Tel: (802) 773-8930
Tel: (800) 526-2778

Japan
Tuttle Publishing
RK Building, 2nd Floor
2-13-10 Shimo-Meguro, Meguro-Ku
Tokyo 153 0064
Tel: (03) 5437-0171
Fax: (03) 5437-0755

Canada
Raincoast Books
8680 Cambie Street
Vancouver, British Columbia
V6P 6M9
Tel: (604) 323-7100
Fax: (604) 323-2600

Southeast Asia
Berkeley Books Pte Ltd
5 Little Road #08-01
Singapore 536983
Tel: (65) 280-1330
Fax: (65) 280-6290

First edition
06 05 04 03 02 01 00   10 9 8 7 6 5 4 3 2 1

Design by Alicia Cech
Printed in the United States of America

Bodhidharma's "The Two Entrances and Four Practices" from *The Roaring Stream: A New Zen Reader*, © 1996 by Nelson Foster and Jack Shoemaker, is reprinted here with their permission.

Table of Contents

Preface   vii

Bodhidharma's *Outline of Practice*   1

Zazen   49

Hakuin and His *Song of Zazen*   69

Sesshin   99

Enlightenment   115

Work and Society   125

Kobe, January 1995   141

Questions and Answers   151

Glossary   177

Preface

SHODO HARADA, the abbot of Sogenji, a three-hundred-year-old Rinzai Zen Temple in Okayama, Japan, is the Dharma heir of Yamada Mumon Roshi (1900–1988), one of the great Rinzai masters of the twentieth century. Harada Roshi offers his teachings to everyone, ordained monks and laypeople, men and women, young and old, from all parts of the world. His students have begun more than a dozen affiliated Zen groups, known as One Drop Zendos, in the United States, Europe, and Asia.

The material that follows was gathered from the newsletters Harada Roshi has prepared for his students, from public talks and talks given during sesshin, and from his answers to questions posed by his students. It is not an academic text but an invitation to practice, compiled from material presented directly to students of all levels of experience. No transcription of the Roshi's words can capture the immediacy of his presence or the full measure of his compassion, but I hope that the simple and straightforward essence of his teaching will hereby be made available to everyone.

Many words from Japanese and other languages for which there are no precise English equivalents are used in the discussion of Zen. Words that are used here only once are defined where they occur; those that appear more than once are given in italics on their first appearance and explained in the Glossary. Many of these words would be rendered with diacritical marks in their original language; for ease of usage, and because many of the terms are finding their way into English without diacritical marks, such marks have been dispensed with here. The names of sutras are given in their most commonly used English form. The names of the Zen ancestors are given in their Japanese forms, as the Roshi speaks them; for the Chinese patriarchs, the Wade-Giles forms of their names are provided in the Glossary.

Many, many people have contributed to this volume. First and foremost, Priscilla Daichi Storandt, in addition to being always at hand to translate the Roshi's words, offered constant and enthusiastic support. Mitra Bishop transcribed tapes, edited many of the newsletters incorporated herein, reviewed drafts of the manuscript, and also provided unfailing encouragement. Thomas Kirchner provided additional translations for and careful editing of the "Zazen" chapter and answered my many questions with good humor and vast knowledge.

Tony Dairyo Fairbank and Jim Whitehill made available copies of material used in this book; Doyu Albin and Shonen Bressler translated passages; Jan Chozen Bays offered advice and guidance; and Brenda Wajun Loew, Lee Paton, Roy Tribelhorn, Eunice Nakao, Domyo, and the many others whom I know only as voices on tapes asked the questions that appear in the final section.

Last but not least, I owe a personal debt of thanks to Tim Jundo Williams, for his constant love and support, and for having encouraged me to go to Japan and meet Shodo Harada Roshi.

—*Jane Lago*

Bodhidharma's *Outline of Practice*

THERE ARE MANY *avenues for entering the Way, but essentially they are all of two kinds: entering through the Principle and entering through practice.*

"Entering through the Principle" is awakening to the essential by means of the teachings. It requires a profound trust that all living beings, both enlightened and ordinary, share the same true nature, which is obscured and unseen due only to mistaken perception. If you turn from the false to the true, dwelling steadily in wall contemplation, there is no self or other, and ordinary people and sages are one and the same. You abide unmoving and unwavering, never again confused by written teachings. Complete, ineffable accord with the Principle is without discrimination, still, effortless. This is called entering through the Principle.

"Entering through practice" refers to four all-encompassing practices: the practice of requiting animosity, the practice of accepting one's circumstances, the practice of craving nothing, and the practice of accord with the Dharma.

What is the practice of requiting animosity? When experiencing suffering, a practitioner of the Way should reflect: "For innumerable eons, I have preferred the superficial to the fundamental, drifting through various states of existence, creating much animosity and hatred, bringing endless harm and discord. Though I have done nothing wrong in this life, I am reaping the natural consequences of past offenses, my evil karma. It is not meted out by some heavenly agency. I accept it patiently and with contentment, utterly without animosity or complaint." *A sutra says,* "When you encounter suffering, do not be distressed. Why? Because your consciousness opens up to the fundamental." Cultivating this attitude, you are in accord with the Principle, advancing on the path through the experience of animosity. Thus it is called the practice of requiting animosity.

Second is the practice of accepting circumstances. Living beings, having no [fixed] self, are entirely shaped by the impact of circumstances. Both suffering and pleasure are produced by circumstances. If you experience such positive rewards as wealth and fame, this results from past causes. You receive the benefits now, but as soon as these circumstances are played out, it will be over. Why should you celebrate? Success and failure depend upon circumstances, while the Mind does not gain or lose. Not being moved even by the winds of good fortune is ineffable accord with the Way. Thus it is called the practice of accepting one's circumstances.

Third is the practice of craving nothing. The various sorts of longing and attachment that people experience in their unending ignorance are regarded as craving. The wise awaken to the truth, going with the Principle rather than with conventional ideas. Peaceful at heart, with nothing to do, they change in accord with the seasons. All existence lacking substance, they desire nothing. [They know that] the goddesses of good and bad fortune always travel as a pair and that the Triple World, where you have lived so long, is like a burning house. Suffering inevitably comes with having a body—who can find peace? If you understand this fully, you quit all thoughts of other states of being, no longer crave them. A sutra says, "To crave is to suffer; to crave nothing is bliss." Thus we understand clearly that craving nothing is the true practice of the Way.

Fourth is the practice of accord with the Dharma. The principle of essential purity is the Dharma. Under this principle, all form is without substance, undefilable and without attachment, neither "this" nor "that." The Vimalakirti Sutra says, "In this Dharma, there are no living beings because it transcends the defil-

BODHIDHARMA'S OUTLINE OF PRACTICE

ing [concept] of 'living beings.' In this Dharma, there is no self because it transcends the defiling [concept] of 'self.'" When the wise embrace and understand this principle, they are practicing accord with the Dharma. Since in the Dharma there is fundamentally nothing to withhold, [the wise] practice generosity, giving their bodies, lives, and possessions without any regret in their minds. Fully understanding the emptiness of giver, gift, and recipient, they do not fall into bias or attachment. Ridding themselves of all defilements, they aid in the liberation of living beings without grasping at appearances. In this way they benefit themselves and others both, gracing the Way of Enlightenment. In the same fashion, they practice the other five perfections. To eliminate false thinking in practicing the six perfections means having no thought of practicing them. This is practicing in accord with the Dharma.

The author of these words, Bodhidharma—known in Japan as Daruma Daishi—is said to have been the third son of Koshi Koku, a king in southern India. Bodhidharma's real name was Bodai Tara, and his older brothers were Getsujo Tara and Kudoku Tara. The following story is told about Bodhidharma:

Hannyatara Sonja—a spiritual teacher whom Bodhidharma's father greatly respected—came to visit the royal palace one day. The king was so moved by Hannyatara Sonja's way of teaching the Dharma that he gave him a jade ball. Hannyatara Sonja showed this ball to the first son of the king, asking him what it was. Getsujo Tara answered, "It is a wonderful ball, unequaled in all the country—a great national treasure." Next, Hannyatara Sonja asked Kudoku Tara how he saw the ball. Kudoku answered, "This is a superb and wonderful jade ball, but if a regular person held it it would have little meaning. Only because you are holding it is it so wonderful." Then he asked Bodai Tara what he thought of the ball. Bodai Tara answered, "This is a wonderful treasure in this world perhaps, but it is not

THE PATH TO BODHIDHARMA

the most important thing. Mind is by far more important. It is like comparing the moon with the sun." Hannyatara Sonja was amazed at the boy's deep understanding.

When, several years later, the king died, Bodai Tara became the disciple of Hannyatara Sonja, who gave him the name Bodhidharma. For forty years Bodhidharma was with his teacher, it is said, and for sixty more he taught, walking all over India. At the end of this time, he knew that conditions were right for him to go to China.

One of the most famous koans in Zen involves the question asked of Master Joshu, "What is the meaning of the Patriarch's coming from the west?" Joshu answered, "The oak tree in the garden." Why did Bodhidharma leave India and go to China? Bodhidharma did not leave India simply to spread enlightenment and teach what he had learned. He had experienced enlightenment and received the transmission directly from the line of Shakyamuni, the Buddha, and his disciple, Makakasho Sonja. One day during his scheduled talk to his students, as we are told in the *Mumonkan*, the Buddha stood on the top of Vulture Peak and simply held up a single flower, and on that day only Makakasho understood. This was the beginning of the transmission, from Shakyamuni's awakening down to the present day. If his teachings had been looked at only as a philosophy, this transmission could never have been passed down. This awakened experience of the Buddha, that which created a path for us to experience, is what the Buddha conveyed that morning; this path cannot be understood only by studying the Buddha's words. In China, before Bodhidharma's time, the people who first studied Buddhism were busy studying the philosophy and teachings of the Buddha and the works of the later Buddhists of India. But these words were not the true teaching; these words just by themselves could not awaken one to the Buddha Nature. What, then, could awaken one to the Buddha

BODHIDHARMA'S *OUTLINE OF PRACTICE*

Nature? This was Bodhidharma's mission, to bring this direct experience to China. Bodhidharma was destined to correctly bring Buddhism to China—not words, but the correct and true essence of Buddhism.

Fifteen hundred years have passed since the time of Bodhidharma. Imagine how difficult it must have been so long ago for such an old man to cross the Indian Ocean, to have faced the wind and the terrible seas in that part of the world. It is said to have taken Bodhidharma nearly three years to reach China; it surely took all of his life energy and strength to make the journey. Bodhidharma had no intention of ever returning to India, but he was not simply looking for another place to teach his Dharma. He knew within that this was what he had to do, beyond any personal desires or needs. Would he actually raise Buddhist disciples in China? He did not know. Would they understand all that he taught? He did not know. How confused were the Chinese about the meaning of the true Dharma? This he could not foresee.

As we live our lives, we encounter many obstructions. These obstructions, like stones in our path, can become sources of confusion, suffering, and pain. It is important that we move beyond them and continue. This is true for everyone, even those who have had a deep enlightenment experience. Even the person who has opened his heart will at times become confused; even those with great wisdom will suffer. Here, a higher training—a greater training—is necessary. This is what Joshu was saying when he answered, "The oak tree in the garden."

Master Rinzai was also asked the question, "What is the meaning of the Patriarch's coming from the west?" He answered, "If there is any meaning at all, you can never save yourself." That is, if there is even the smallest bit of self-awareness left in our minds, we cannot be content, and we cannot say we are liberated. Yet if we have no self-awareness, no consciousness, how do we take on social obligations? If we have no self-awareness left in our minds, how do we go about living our lives? Such questions naturally arise when we look at these words of Rinzai.

"If there is any meaning at all, you can never save yourself." This is not an intellectual problem. Rinzai is saying that if you take the question up intellectually, you will never get it. In fact, you will be doing what all the scholars and social theorists are doing. There is essentially no difference. But how can we then say that Bodhidharma did not have self-awareness? How can we say that we should not be working consciously when we are out in the world? How can we go about living our lives so that we will not be caught by our own thoughts and fantasies when we are out there functioning in the world? What is Rinzai saying? This is what we are all trying to know, and what Bodhidharma taught.

According to the *Transmission of the Lamp*, Bodhidharma reached China in the year A.D. 527. The emperor at the time was Wu, the founder of the Liang dynasty. Emperor Wu was known as a strong supporter of Buddhism because of his great efforts in providing for the copying and distribution of sutras, in bringing monks and priests to his realm, in building thousands of temples, and in training tens of thousands of monks. By doing these things, he hoped to raise the spirituality of his countrymen. When he heard that Bodhidharma was coming, he looked forward to meeting him and awaited him eagerly.

When Bodhidharma arrived, the emperor said, "I've built many temples, given livelihood to tens of thousands of monks, and translated many sutras. What is the merit from this?"

Bodhidharma answered, "No merit."

No matter how many temples or monks the emperor asked about, "No merit" was the answer he received from Bodhidharma.

BODHIDHARMA'S *OUTLINE OF PRACTICE*

It is easy to misunderstand Bodhidharma's answer. What is he really saying? When we do our zazen, is it really of no merit? If there is the slightest speck of thought as to what will be gained through this practice, such a clouded view will get us nowhere. At the same time, if we do not vow to attain enlightenment, how can we get there?

If you are thinking about these questions all the time, you still have far to go. As Joshu wrote, "The dog's Buddha-nature: Offer up yourself from the tips of your toes to the very top of your head!" If there is the slightest awareness of good or bad, you are as good as dead. If you are still aware of your breathing and your body, the zazen of no merit is far away. When you experience the mind without a single speck of clutter, you will, for the first time, experience the zazen of no merit. Bodhidharma answered "No merit" and said it all. If you want to do wonderful things—build temples, raise disciples, translate sutras—go ahead. But if there is even one speck of self-awareness in your doing of these things, then it is all impure.

The emperor was shocked at Bodhidharma's response and asked, "Building temples, raising disciples, and translating sutras—if these are all of no merit, then what is most important in the world? If these are all meaningless, where is the deepest meaning to be found?"

Bodhidharma answered, "Nothing holy, only emptiness."

Nothing splendid. Only emptiness everywhere, like that vast fall sky. Not a speck of anything to be grateful for. We all have to sit until we can experience this. We must sit straight like Mount Fuji rising out of the sea and do zazen that raises our entire body and touches our deepest center! Foggy, vague zazen will not do. Unless we can become taut and full it will be useless. Yet even that is not good enough if any trace of self-conscious awareness remains. We have to be rid of it all. Bodhidharma said, "Nothing holy, only emptiness." We have to sit until we know this essence for ourselves.

The emperor was again shocked and asked, "Who is answering the emperor like this?!"

Bodhidharma said, "I don't know."

The emperor could not understand these words spoken by Bodhidharma. So Bodhidharma left Emperor Wu's land and traveled north to a mountain called Sozan near present-day Beijing, where he was given a temple.

It is said that, at this temple, Shorinji, Bodhidharma just sat for nine years, but probably he did not simply sit. For at this temple he had a student, Niso Eka, the second Chinese patriarch. If Bodhidharma had not raised a disciple, the Dharma would not have continued. Many guests came to the temple with questions for Bodhidharma, the answers to which he left in a collection of writings. One brief part of those writings is his *Ni Nyu Shi Gyo Kan*—his teaching called *Outline of Practice*, also known as *On the Twofold Entrance to the Tao* or *The Two Entrances and Four Practices*, which we are reading here. So, clearly, Bodhidharma was not just doing zazen.

As a young monk, Niso Eka was a scholar. He had studied for many years and mastered the scriptures, but in his heart he was never able to be secure. Dissatisfied with what he could discover through his intellect, he went to see Bodhidharma, to ask for his help and guidance.

Bodhidharma was a very strict master and very strict on himself. No matter how much physical strain or suffering he experienced, he never took his mind off the wall in front of him; he sat and sat, facing the wall. But he was not wasting a minute in doing this—he was in the true practice of no gaps. In our daily life we leave many pauses unfilled; for Bodhidharma, it was natural to return immediately to the cushion—to return immediately to zazen—after a meal, after completing a task, whenever there was open time. Throughout the ages, many Buddhists have

BODHIDHARMA'S OUTLINE OF PRACTICE

lived this way, so that zazen is always continuing, in life and back on the cushion.

Many words have been written describing the suffering state of Niso Eka when he went to call on Bodhidharma at Shorinji in early December. In the area of China near Beijing the weather is extremely cold at that time of the year. Yet on that winter evening, the middle-aged Niso Eka stood outside Bodhidharma's temple, in the blowing snow. His studies had been thorough, but he still had doubt; he had practiced zazen for eight years, but he could not find solace in his practice. He had heard of Bodhidharma's arrival in China and that he taught not any special morality, or any special virtue, but only sitting, facing the wall.

When Niso Eka arrived at the temple, Bodhidharma was sitting as usual on his cushion. It snowed and snowed, but Bodhidharma just sat quietly without even turning around. And Niso Eka waited, standing in the snow that was piling up nearly to his waist. He made his best efforts at this time, his greatest efforts to cut all of his thoughts, to be ready to finally encounter the true teaching.

Finally, Bodhidharma answered the door. He looked down on Niso Eka, standing in the snow, and asked him, "You have long been standing in the snow. What are you here for? What are you seeking?"

Niso Eka replied, "I came to learn the true Dharma. I came to find true faith. Please, Bodhidharma, have compassion and teach me, teach us, the truth." In tears, he pleaded with Bodhidharma.

Bodhidharma told him, "The true path is not so easy to get to. You will not get there just like that. With your knowledge in your head, you will never get there. With only belief, you will never get there. The Truth is at the Source of all beings; but if any shadow of information and learning is still there, you will never be able to see it. It is best that you stop your searching right now."

This encounter is recorded in the *Transmission of the Lamp*, but we do not know how accurate the account really is. The story was most likely embellished. It continues, saying that Niso Eka then took out a knife and, having let go of all attachments to his body, cut off his left arm and presented it to Bodhidharma. We do not know if this really happened, but we do know that Niso Eka was very sincere when he traveled to find Bodhidharma, and that he was indeed ready to put his life on the line.

Niso Eka, through eight years of doing zazen, had deepened to a place we can hardly understand nowadays, but we know that at times we can feel a power of will and enthusiasm similar to his. It is difficult to manifest that will for practice, but a new monk in the monastery traditionally is taught something of this effort. He sits for days outside the gates, not being allowed in. Then, when he is finally allowed inside the temple, he is put into a room where he must meditate for days, not knowing what will happen. He does not know when, or how many times, he will be thrown out of the temple again and forced to try to reenter. A new monk entering the monastery is tested in this way for up to seven days. It is possible that this tradition, still followed today, derives from this legacy of Bodhidharma and Niso Eka and their first encounter.

Niso Eka had asked Bodhidharma to teach him of the Buddha's mind and was unrelenting in showing his deep and true resolve. He had come to know that this Mind of the Buddha was something no one else could give him. His thoughts were keeping him far away, and he was desperate for help.

Bodhidharma clearly knew that people often become discouraged and give up before reaching the resolution of their practice, pulled away by ideas, mistaking them for the real thing.

BODHIDHARMA'S *OUTLINE OF PRACTICE*

Or they become conceited and overly self-assured, straying far from the path to enlightenment. When Bodhidharma saw Niso Eka cutting off his arm, he said to him, "Buddhas, when they first seek after the truth, give no heed to their bodies for the sake of the Dharma. You have now cut off your arm before me, and have shown your sincerity and your seeking."

Niso Eka replied, "Until now I have studied how to live, I have studied the Tao, I have studied the sutras, and I know the path very well, but I am not satisfied deep inside. After all that endless study, I still cannot find true peace of mind anywhere!" He was asking Bodhidharma for help, for the courage to awaken himself.

Niso Eka was brilliant; even as a child he had been able to read the most difficult philosophical texts. Even when he was young he was looking for some word of advice on awakening, but this is something that does not come easily. With a well-studied mind come images and ideas that are always blocking the true light. Those ideas are not necessary. If you are settled in your heart, you do not have to think, you do not have to worry whether you exist or not, you do not have to pursue any such philosophical questions. This was Bodhidharma's truth.

Niso Eka said to Bodhidharma, "Your disciple's mind is not yet at peace. I beg of you, my teacher, please give it peace."

Bodhidharma said, "Bring your mind to me, and I will set it at rest."

Bodhidharma's answer was so sharp. Penetrating to the core, he tried to point Niso Eka to the root of all his problems. Niso Eka was wise in thought and words, and in using his head, but Bodhidharma did not allow any room for that at all—he cut through it, getting to the final place right away. Bodhidharma was always living with his life right out there on the line, without the slightest excess; if that had not been the case, he could not have answered like this.

THE PATH TO BODHIDHARMA

We do not know how long Niso Eka tried to do as he was asked. Eventually he said to Bodhidharma, "I have searched for the mind, and it is finally unattainable."

Bodhidharma replied, "I have thoroughly set it at rest for you."

At that moment Niso Eka attained deep enlightenment. He realized his deepest mind. If he had not just gone through all of that pain, it would not have happened when Bodhidharma responded as he did. Niso Eka realized his own clear mind and in one moment melted his burden of doubt.

Bodhidharma's words—"I have thoroughly set it at rest for you"— are clear; they are not the words of a scholar. It took Shakyamuni six years to attain this understanding; before his enlightenment, Shakyamuni was taught by his last teacher that the True Mind finally, in the end, has no thought. If we do not come to know this, we will never be able to appease our doubts. Yet Shakyamuni was able to see beyond this point. He had the energy to cut all of his thoughts; yet he questioned deeper. "What about daily life? When I go out into the world, what if I need food, what about the mind then? My mind then cannot just be the mind of no thoughts. There must be something else." True, in the essence of the mind there is no thought, but this was not Shakyamuni's final realization. He knew he would have to work harder, work longer, and take it to the very end. It took Mumon Ekai six years to finally understand. It took Niso Eka eight. It is not easy to understand the words of Bodhidharma. Niso Eka said, "I have searched for the mind, and it is finally unattainable." He had come to a very good place and worked very hard, or he would not have been able to say this. It took him many years to reach this place. Perhaps the shadows were all gone and his thoughts had all disappeared, perhaps there was nothing left there. He had comprehended this point, and Bodhidharma saw his purity. Niso Eka had reached the very

BODHIDHARMA'S OUTLINE OF PRACTICE

roots of his mind when he approached Bodhidharma and said, "I have searched for the mind, and it is finally unattainable."

"I have thoroughly set it at rest for you," Bodhidharma said. There, that is it; if you look there, that is it. Bodhidharma cut right through what remained of Niso Eka's thoughts. We all have to be able to achieve that clear cutting edge of Bodhidharma—no body, no mind, nothing anywhere, nothing but that clear place: "I have thoroughly set it at rest for you." It is that simple. As Shakyamuni was also teaching us, if we meet that true Source completely, if we know our true living minds, then no thoughts are necessary. Rinzai, too, received that clear teaching from his teacher, Obaku. We all have to believe and come to see this.

In his *Outline of Practice*, Bodhidharma teaches the true and correct way of the mind. Mumon Ekai said, "The Great Way is without a gate." It is not some small path but the Great Way of heaven and earth! And yet there is no such visible way.

Joshu was asked, "What is the Way?"

He answered, "Just outside that gate runs Route 2, which goes to Tokyo."

This is not just any old path—this Great Path of no gate with no planned shape! You can enter everywhere. It can be confusing because the possibilities are many. However, as Bodhidharma tells us, this path can generally be divided into two main divisions.

The first entrance to the path is by reason, or "through the Principle":

"Entering through the Principle" is awakening to the essential by means of the teachings. It requires a profound trust that all living beings, both enlightened and ordinary, share the same true nature, which is obscured and unseen due only to mistaken perception. If you turn from the false to the true, dwelling steadily in wall contemplation, there is no self or other, and ordinary people

and sages are one and the same. You abide unmoving and unwavering, never again confused by written teachings. Complete, ineffable accord with the Principle is without discrimination, still, effortless. This is called entering through the Principle.

There is a phrase, "to hear one and understand ten." This refers to an ability to grasp, without words of explanation, exactly what is being said. When those of true, deep practice hear just a bit, right away they know the whole thing and exactly how to proceed. The first way is to go directly, straightforwardly, without looking around, needing no prompts, no zazen—just aiming for *kensho* with no other needs whatsoever.

Rinzai never said to do zazen. Only to realize kensho—this is Rinzai's Zen. And if we do not do it now, if we do not attain enlightenment at this very time, then for the infinite amount of time that exists, the mind of the Buddha, with which we are all endowed, will never be awakened to. This is said by Rinzai very severely and very clearly. He said only to go ahead directly and straightforwardly, and you will know without asking how each day should be lived. If we can reach that understanding once, we will understand the rest without problems. This is the first entrance of which Bodhidharma speaks. This is how the sixth patriarch did it.

Can you hear the Dharma of this very moment? What is there to listen to right now? Is the Dharma in people's explanations? Will speaking words of kindness be thought of as the teaching of the Dharma? Right here, right now, hearing the drum go boom, hearing the ring of the sutra gong—or even the sound of the book page turning—what is it that hears this? Directly and clearly experience that, and then there will be nothing left to seek; for your whole life you will live as a true person. Rinzai taught this time and time again: That which hears the boom of the drum—this is neither man nor woman, young nor old, rich nor poor, neither scholar nor an uneducated person, not

BODHIDHARMA'S *OUTLINE OF PRACTICE*

square and not round, not red and not white—it is simply one True Person of No Rank and only that. It is not form or substance and has no standing at all. It is that which becomes our eyes and sees, becomes our ears and hears, becomes our nose and smells, and becomes our mouth and tastes. It is that which becomes our hands and can hold things, becomes our feet and can carry our body. Rinzai would say, "Do you still not understand?"

We do not experience kensho merely from our energy of the Way, nor can we experience it from not trying anything at all. If our zazen power is strong we will attain enlightenment without fail. This is how it works. But it will not do to make kensho into a concept. The word *kensho* is constantly on our tongues, but if we think there is some kind of change waiting to happen to us, or that we will become some other kind of person, we are in for a big surprise. Instead, our mind becomes perfectly clear—that which is speaking, hearing, and seeing just as it is is kensho. This mind—we cannot see it, but we know it. First and foremost, if you realize your Original Nature, the way that things should be done in society will become clear and obvious.

The second entrance Bodhidharma speaks of can be found within our daily lives—eating, going to the bathroom, moving our arms and legs. We can realize it in life's very midst. This is Entering through Practice, or Entering through Conduct. And if our conduct is truly correct conduct, we naturally enter "through the Principle" as well.

The four parts of Entering through Practice listed by Bodhidharma include and encompass all others. The first is to know how to receive hatred and yet know also how to requite it. This is the practice of requiting animosity. The second is to follow our karma with acceptance and without resistance. This is the practice of accepting circumstances. The third is to not desire anything or wish for anything external. This is the practice of craving nothing. We wish for things outside ourselves because we are lonely and missing something within. But if we are truly fulfilled and taut within, we are not lonely in this way and need nothing else. The fourth part is the practice of accord with the Dharma. This means to live each minute of each day in accordance with the Dharma.

To arrive at the gate of Zen, wanting to realize our deepest profound mind—if this is what we are truly searching for we should remind ourselves of the following:

When experiencing suffering, a practitioner of the Way should reflect: "For innumerable eons, I have preferred the superficial to the fundamental, drifting through various states of existence, creating much animosity and hatred, bringing endless harm and discord. Though I have done nothing wrong in this life, I am reaping the natural consequences of past offenses, my evil karma. It is not meted out by some heavenly agency. I accept it patiently and with contentment, utterly without animosity or complaint." A sutra says, "When you encounter suffering, do not be distressed. Why? Because your consciousness opens up to the fundamental." Cultivating this attitude, you are in accord with the Principle, advancing on the path through the experience of animosity. Thus it is called the practice of requitting animosity.

We often think—mistakenly—that we receive life in our first cry at birth. This is an easy illusion and one that occurs frequently. But if we look more closely, we can see it is not like this. We have not sprung from the earth and the rocks. We have come from the living bodies of our mother and father. Is our life separate from theirs? Of course not. Our life comes from theirs, and if we look back through time into the endless past, we find a connection to all of our ancestors, and even beyond that. More than four billion years ago the earth was born. It is said that one million years ago or so human life as we know it appeared on the earth. That means it took many millions of years for this very life to be given birth to. Our life, the life that we are expressing right now, did not easily appear in one moment. We did not come to be living here so simply, so coincidentally. Our life is part of a continuous line of hundreds of millions of years. We are at this history's present point, expressed at its fullest in this very moment. And that is only looking at it from the point of view of the age of this earth. If humans originally came from another planet or celestial body, we may have an even greater amount of history behind us.

Science teaches us about many life-forms that existed before humans. Embryonically we can see similarities between humans and amoebas, fish, birds, and all animals. In the months and days of pregnancy, this development of millions of years is condensed into a short period. What were our ancestors—the birds, the fish, the amoebas—doing during the millions of years that passed before humans emerged on this planet? Were the strong eating the weak in order to survive? Probably we ate a good many living others in order to bring about this life today. This is how we came to be present in this living form.

Looking realistically at the history of mankind, we can see that, simply to preserve our existence, we have left so much to our instincts. And because of that we have the civilization that is here today. Did we all do such good things? Of course not. Because we left everything to instinct there were wars and struggles. History teaches this clearly. Finally, twenty-five hundred years ago, the Buddha's teaching came forth. Two thousand years ago came the teachings of Christ, Socrates, and Confucius. At around the same time they all appeared and finally offered a guiding light to humanity. Maybe there were glimpses before this, but no one carried them on.

Look at the world today: We are constantly threatened by war. We have just become a little more clever; that's all. On this earth, this civilization that lets its instincts lead has taken many lives. We call ourselves the most highly developed culture now, but we also bear responsibility for the evil deeds of all those lives of the past: hate, ill will, wrongdoing, limitless mistaken behavior. Even if we can say we have not done anything mistaken or evil in the years of this present body, compared to the entire history of human beings this is a very short time. Even if we can say that we have not harmed or bothered anyone from the time of our birth to the present, that is relatively a very brief interval. Think it over carefully. In this world, when we experience our own suffering, we should look at it in this way.

Bodhidharma has a very severe perspective on this: No one can foretell what will happen next. The deeds of the past are bearing fruit right now, in this very moment. Neither the heavens nor the gods nor others can be held responsible. It is all from my own deeds in the past that I experience these results right now. Our life is not just from the moment of this birth. If we are living and suffering now, accept that we are experiencing the consequences of our own doings in the past, and do not hold it against others.

When we fall into evil-doing and mistaken behavior in society, we are called responsible and are blamed by others. But those who understand profoundly the deepest paths know that we have reached the true and solid character of human beings when we realize that we must throw away the stingy idea of not accepting our own behavior. If we can see this, no matter what happens to us, we can accept it, we can say, "Even if people of society do not know, I do." We must clearly be able to say that we have understood where this responsibility lies, and not just say it after justice has been decided by others. If we are truly clear in our state of mind, then we will let what has come be as it is. This attitude is identical in Christianity and Buddhism.

In a house near the temple of Shoinji in the town of Hara, where Master Hakuin Zenji lived, the daughter became pregnant. Her father was furious and demanded to know who the father of her baby was. Knowing that her father respected Hakuin and was always talking about him, she answered that Hakuin was the baby's father, hoping that would keep her father quiet. The father became even angrier, shocked at this respected priest's behavior. When the baby was born, he took it to Hakuin, yelling at him and accusing him. Knowing something was behind the father's behavior, Hakuin accepted the child, saying, "Yes? Yes?" He took the baby in, never defending himself. He had to find places for the baby to be nursed. When he would go on *takuhatsu*, his begging rounds, people would point at him and talk behind his back. He even wrote a letter saying that the rumors had become so burdensome that he could no longer go outside.

Finally, the young mother's mind became so weighted down with what she had done that she confessed that the father of her child was in fact another neighborhood man, and tried to apologize. Her father, even more furious at the shame she had brought on the family, went to Hakuin and apologized profusely, thinking of course that Hakuin would be very angry. But Hakuin only answered "Yes? Yes?" and returned the baby. During that time he never defended himself or accused others. It takes a truly great person of the Way like Hakuin to be able to do something like this.

When Furuna Sonja, a disciple of the Buddha, was preparing to go far away to spread the Buddha's teachings, the Buddha asked him, "Where you are going they have no culture. They will kick you and strike you and spit in your face. Is that OK with you?"

His disciple said, "I think about it like this: Even if they hit me and kick me and spit on me, they will not take my life."

Then the Buddha said, "They might even take your life; is that still all right with you?"

THE PATH TO BODHIDHARMA

At that his disciple said, "At that time I will think like this: They are liberating me from my body, the physical source of my great suffering and grief."

The Buddha said, "Then go there. If you have confidence and resolution like this, there is no mistake."

This is the first of the four parts of Entering through Practice, the practice of requiting animosity. Bodhidharma is telling us about this very clearly, not to confuse us but to encourage us to accept this truth in our everyday lives.

Ryokan says in a poem:

To meet disaster at the time of disaster is fine just as it is.
To meet illness in the time of illness is fine just as it is.
To meet death at the time of death is fine just as it is.

Disaster and illness, being alive every day and then dying—these are all passing varieties of scenery. Once we know their source and their transience, we will not be caught by them, we will be able to remain unmoved by pain and by pleasure. That clean, pure mind of zazen shows us the way things truly are in society, in the world around us. It is all synchronicity. When we can live our everyday life in this way, knowing this is like kensho. The sutras teach us that when we receive others' revenge and suffer through torturous worlds, we should receive it all just as it is—and not only that, but make it into our foundation and live from that place and express ourselves from that Great Mind beyond all attachments. If we can accept the difficulties and use them in our own favor, not running away from them but following them, we will certainly come to enlightenment.

A story is told about a large temple called Zuiganji in Sendai, and about the person who became the first abbot there, Hoshin Kokushi. In the nearby area of Makabe there was a castle, and in the castle a servant by the name of Heshiro was responsible for taking care of the *daimyo's geta*—the lord's footwear. One night, Heshiro accompanied the daimyo as he went out for the evening. But when the daimyo reached his destination, Heshiro was not allowed to go inside with the daimyo because he was only a servant. It was a very cold night in Makabe. As was the custom, the daimyo left his shoes outside as he entered the building. Because he did not want the daimyo to have to put cold geta on his feet, Heshiro warmed the shoes in his coat. Just before the daimyo was ready to leave, Heshiro returned the geta to the building's entrance. When the daimyo came out and found that his geta were warm, he was furious and accused Heshiro of having sat on them. The daimyo was irate at Heshiro's kindness; everything had gotten turned around. He was so furious he threw the geta at Heshiro, who grabbed them and ran away. Heshiro went to Kyoto, where he remained enraged at his miserable situation, thinking only about what he could do to get back at the daimyo. They were both equal as human beings on this earth, so why should he have been put into such a miserable position? He decided to become ordained, because that was the one way he could get the daimyo to bow down to him.

In those days one had to go to China to become ordained, so Heshiro stowed away on a ship. When he arrived in China, he went to a *dojo* on Kinzan Mountain, but he could not understand a word that was said there. He could not read, either—having been only a servant he had never learned any *kanji*. This troubled the Kinzan roshi. Heshiro was a very enthusiastic student, and the roshi wanted to do something for him. Then the roshi had an idea. He drew a huge circle with a big J in the middle and asked Heshiro what it was. Heshiro did zazen day and night trying to figure out what the circle and the J meant. He had been deeply injured by the daimyo's insults, and he trained desperately—harder than anyone else. Maybe there was no meaning in that circle with the J in it, but through his deep efforts he reached enlightenment doing zazen on this drawing. That one deep thought of anger and revenge at the daimyo brought him to this great understanding; finally he was able to drop it all, to lose all sense of inner and outer, his whole sense of self and other, earth and heavens, until, like a huge explosion, it all fell away. He could not understand the drawing, but everything around him appeared illumined. After that he returned to Kyoto and to the temple of Myoshinji.

Zuiganji, the temple in Sendai, which was near Makabe, had just been made into a dojo of the Myoshinji line, and Heshiro was sent there to establish it as a training monastery. A great ceremony was held in his honor as the new abbot. All the royalty lined up along the path to the entrance of the *hondo*, where Heshiro was to offer a poem expressing his understanding, as is customary at such times.

The daimyo had forgotten Heshiro's face, of course. The abbot's poem was about having climbed Mount Kinzan in China, having done many years of practice and finally realizing true understanding, and then coming down from Kinzan to this faraway place of training. It was about how our physical bodies are made up of the Five Elements, of sadness and joy, so that if we look at them through awakened eyes we need no property, no fame or great name. We can see that they have no meaning and rise out of emptiness. He concluded by saying that now the Buddha Nature had returned to open this new dojo and bring sentient beings to enlightenment.

After that it was time for the daimyo to do prostrations to Heshiro, who was now the daimyo's teacher. Heshiro laid out grass on a tall tray, and on the same tray carefully laid out those very same geta that the daimyo had thrown at him. The daimyo entered, but still he did not understand what had happened. The new abbot came down off his cushion and bowed to the daimyo, saying that although the daimyo had probably forgotten who he was, he—who was formerly Heshiro—had not been able to forget. Then he described the incident of the geta in detail, and told the daimyo that those same geta were on the tray before them. He told how he had trained with all his energy just so he could get the daimyo to bow to him, but when he thought about it carefully, it was thanks to the daimyo's anger that he had gone into training at all. If it had not been for that, he would have remained the daimyo's servant for the rest of his life. If the daimyo had not been furious at him, he would never have become abbot that day. He bowed in thanks to the daimyo. The daimyo was, of course, astonished at hearing all of this.

In society, justice is of great importance. Today we have courts for that reason. We have to pay our debts; in society this is a matter of course. But we must ask if this is the only way. How can we make up for our own mistakes? We have courts to settle disputes, yet still there are fights and still we have wars. In society that is considered normal. But is it right to take people's lives for the sake of justice? Is that the best possible solution, the only possible solution?

There is another way. If we follow the way of Zen, first we become Buddhists, and then we awaken not only ourselves but all others. The Buddha showed us this by his example. In his own life, before his very eyes, he saw his parents die and his country fall to ruin. But the Buddha saw through all of this. He saw that the actual truth could not be destroyed, that it was not a matter of winning or losing or of being happy for one brief period of time. Buddhism is the Way that teaches us this eternal truth. This Way is not a transient way. It is the ultimate resolution, not a temporary one. We must heed the teaching of this Way.

No matter how long we take various roundabout paths in our lives, at some point we must realize our Buddha Nature.

THE PATH TO BODHIDHARMA

For this we have been walking always, with all of civilization. In the ultimate world we will all be in this way of Zen. Why not do it right now instead of waiting until tomorrow and starting over from the beginning? The teachings of the Buddha and of Bodhidharma are all for this, for doing it now, right away.

Bodhidharma teaches that the second part of *Entering through Practice* is about being obedient to karma. This is called accepting circumstances.

Living beings, having no [fixed] self, are entirely shaped by the impact of circumstances. Both suffering and pleasure are produced by circumstances. If you experience such positive rewards as wealth and fame, this results from past causes. You receive the benefits now, but as soon as these circumstances are played out, it will be over. Why should you celebrate? Success and failure depend upon circumstances, while the Mind does not gain or lose. Not being moved even by the winds of good fortune is ineffable accord with the Way. Thus it is called the practice of accepting one's circumstances.

No matter what happens, what is most important is to accept it all and respond accordingly, moving correctly in our daily lives. We must become as accepting as a newborn baby. None of us thought to be born into this world, at this time, to these parents. We received from the source, totally and innocently, the circumstances into which we were born, with no expectations, no knowledge, and no preconceptions about what this life would be like when we entered it. We accepted our situation of birth. We never thought about how we would not want to be born into this difficult-to-live-in house, into this period of history. After the term of pregnancy we are merely born, and we arrive, with a big cry and total acceptance. Our mother's, father's, and ancestors' habits are given to us without our expectation. Therefore, to say "This is good" and "This is bad" is to add something on afterward—it is not something that is part of

BODHIDHARMA'S *OUTLINE OF PRACTICE*

our pure mind at birth.

Were we not pure when we were first born? No one comes out of the womb complaining about having to be born—that is what Bodhidharma is saying. In this part he is teaching that we are fundamentally without any egoistic self whatsoever. The baby accepts the world with which it is presented without judgment, exactly as the world is presented. Adults are always judging and complaining. Which is the easier way to live?

When our minds are free from egoistic views, we can accept things exactly as they are. We can see everything with our eyes because our eyes are empty; they no longer take double exposures. As one thing leaves, then the next thing appears. My teacher, Mumon Roshi, used to tell a funny story about someone looking in the mirror one morning and noticing that she had a wrinkled face and white hair all of a sudden. Upon investigation, she found that her grandmother had just used the mirror, and her image was still reflected there. Of course, mirrors do not act like that. Nor do our eyes. Only our egoistic consciousness does this, and this is unfortunate.

We have the teaching of Bankei on the Unborn Buddha Nature. He would say that when people came to see him, they came expecting to hear him speak. But if a dog were to bark at the same time, they would hear that dog bark as well, without having had any expectation of hearing the barking of a dog right then. Even though the mind is empty, void of any intention of hearing a dog barking—there is no idea about it in there at all—you still hear the dog when it barks. This empty mind that hears the dog barking is the Unborn Buddha Nature, this mind that works with no expectation or preparation or plan. Our True Mind is empty of ego, like a baby's mind.

To realize this mind we use the breathing practice of *susokkan* or the Mu koan of Master Joshu: "A monk asked Master Joshu, 'Does a dog have Buddha Nature?' Master Joshu answered 'MU!'" But if we are saying Mu all the time, does it mean we are empty and pure? If I call a person in *sanzen* a fool, that person becomes angry immediately. Where does that anger come from if the person is so empty? To do zazen until the Mu flows and circulates throughout the body and mind, that is all that can be done. In our minds we know what Mu should be, but to realize it, to become it, is not so easy. We must do it not just in the *zendo* but eating, standing, and working—if we can keep that Mu going always, then no matter what comes along, we have only Mu to meet it with. Although we are pure from the origin, we still have physical bodies; we still have to eat and sleep. But our physical bodies are merely borrowed utensils for the purpose of realizing our Buddha Nature. In truth, there is nothing but mind, which is completely clear. Not even a name can be placed here. That which sees the red flower or the green willow and hears the dog barking is the same for each of us who sees and hears it. If we say it sounds different in different languages, that is already putting on to it the dualism of language and separating ourselves from it. Every person is born with this mind from the origin, which is Mu. Anyone can realize this.

Yet we are all different in our physical characteristics, possessions, intelligence, and personality. Why are we all so different? All children spend a long time wondering about this one! Bodhidharma teaches that of course we are different. Our parents are all different, our parents' personalities are all different, and their parents' personalities as well. We are not little rolls or croissants being made exactly alike at the bakery each day. We have our father's personality and also the karma of being born from him. We have our mother's personality and also the karma of being born from her. Why does the person next to me come from such a rich family? No matter how much I worry about it, it will not make any difference. All of our differences come from karmic connections reaching back long before our own birth.

BODHIDHARMA'S *OUTLINE OF PRACTICE*

Originally, our source is without stain, empty of egoistic self. But why, then, we wonder, do we suffer so? There are even some who suffer all the time; they live in the midst of constant suffering, unable to do anything about it, while other people are living in happiness and comfort. Everything comes from karmic connections, and everything will eventually change when the karmic effects that brought it about wear off.

Near Uwajima in Imamatsu there was a family of long standing—ten or more generations—named Konishi. This was a family of sake makers and among the ten richest families in all of Japan. One day, the father of the first generation went into town, and on his return he rested along the way with a big barrel of sake next to him. A samurai came walking toward him, sweating and tired. The sake maker's barrel was full of sake, and the samurai could smell it. He asked for a drink because he was so thirsty.

First the sake maker took out a little plate. Using some leaves he gathered nearby, he sprinkled sake in the four directions; then he gave two other offerings as well. The samurai asked him what he was doing. The sake maker said that he had just opened a new sake barrel and was thanking all the gods in the four directions, and the daimyo as well, with his offerings. The samurai understood thanking the gods, but why, he asked, was the sake maker thanking the daimyo? The sake maker answered, "Because the daimyo keeps the country in peace so the sake can be made. We always thank him before taking the first drink out of the sake barrel."

The samurai, who was of high rank in Uwajima Castle, returned to the daimyo and told him what had happened. The daimyo made the sake maker into the royal sake maker who provided all the sake to the castle, and he became very famous and his sake very popular. For many generations his family continued to hold this position, until the time in history came when the current sake maker had to give up his home, his lands, and all of his possessions to the country. When the karmic connection is finished, everything changes. All circumstances are only borrowed; good things, bad things, suffering, joy—all come out of past karma. So there is nothing to be so proud or so happy about. If you see the present reality clearly, you will not be tossed and turned about by current conditions, knowing they are only transient and will change.

It is easy to see this in times of suffering—in the tough times, especially, we can believe that those conditions will change. But when the winds of good fortune and wealth begin to blow, how weak we become! We so easily become proud and feel rewarded and comfortable in our circumstances. Knowing there is only one kind of karma, no matter what comes along, we must realize the truth and follow the path; whether our karma is good or bad, we must not drown in it. We should become obedient to our karma, accepting all circumstances, as Bodhidharma writes in this section. "It is easier for a camel to go through the eye of a needle, than for a rich man to enter into the kingdom of God"—this is how it is written in the Bible.

There was once a very, very rich family named Tajima. There was a strict rule in this family, however, that when each year's rice harvest came in, only what the family needed was to be kept—all the rest was to be given away. The rule was never to build storehouses or warehouses, but to give rice to all the temples and shrines and to the poor people. When the end of the Tokugawa era came, the daimyo ran out of money and asked everyone to give something from the wealth in their stores. The Tajima family had no money at all—they had given all of their rice and profits away. This was known by everyone; it was known that they could not give money. The government, too, was aware of this and did not ask them for anything. Other great houses went broke, but the Tajima family had known from the begin-

BODHIDHARMA'S *OUTLINE OF PRACTICE*

ning that it was all borrowed profit.

In Zen there is the teaching of the half scoopful of water. In the monastery each morning, three small bamboo scoops full of water are allowed to wash the face and to rinse the mouth out, and the last half of the third scoop is always returned to the water source. We continue this practice of not wasting water today, even though we now have running water in the monasteries.

At Sogenji there is the story of the master whose bathwater was far too hot. He told the disciple who was in charge of the bath that day to bring some cold water. At that time, of course, there was no faucet to make the water start running. The disciple had to go all the way out to the well, pull up a bucketful of water, take the water into the bath, and then go back to the well again to bring up another bucketful of water, and go back into the bath with it. Many times he went back and forth from the well bringing cold water. When the bath was finally cooled to just the right temperature, the master said, "Okay, that's good enough."

When he said "that's good enough," the monk took the little bit of water that was left in the bucket and dumped it out on the floor. He put the bucket upside down and, thinking his work was finished, prepared to leave. His teacher was furious and said, "What are you doing?" The monk was amazed and did not understand why, when he had just finished his job, his teacher was suddenly angry at him. The master said, "You thought there was only a little bit of water left in that bucket, so you dumped it out so carelessly. Why, just because it was a little bit of water, did you not perceive how to give that little bit of water life? If you had taken it outside you could have put it on a flower, you could have given it to a tree, you could have used it for the vegetables in the garden."

The master knew and was telling the monk that in one

drop of water, even in the slightest drop of water, there is an entire universe of energy and functioning. We must make our efforts so that we are using what comes to us totally—if there is a lot of water we can use it in a big way, but with even the smallest drop of water we should put our efforts totally into taking the life of that one drop seriously and using it in the best possible way. That is what doing our practice is all about.

There are four major temples of Myoshinji, for whom there were four big pine trees planted, which are still growing at Myoshinji today. A story that comes from the time of the planting of those pines tells us that at that time one of the Myoshinji priests was traveling near Lake Biwa. It was a very hot day, and he saw the cool-looking water. One man was swimming in the water, a second man was bathing himself in the water, a third man was washing himself on the bank at the edge of the water, and a fourth man was washing himself with a towel that had been dampened in the water. The meaning of this story is that we can easily jump into the water and swim and bathe. But the priest—being the one who had the most understanding—said, "I don't have the merit to use the water like this; some must be left for those who come later. If I do what is easiest and use up all the water now, what will be left for generations to come?"

The same is true for our pollution problem today; if everyone thought like this priest, there would be no problem. If we think that our life is only from the moment we are born until the moment we die, we are making a big mistake. We exist from the very beginning of our history, one million years ago. The straight line that comes down from that moment through now—this is my life! And this moment is the ultimate point of it, right now. Every being breathing the air and drinking the water on this planet, on this earth, is my life as well. If a big bomb drops, it is over for all of us. The earth is turning, and the radiation will fall everywhere.

BODHIDHARMA'S *OUTLINE OF PRACTICE*

Remember, as Bodhidharma tells us, "Living beings, having no [fixed] self, are entirely shaped by the impact of circumstances." We have to perceive this Buddha Nature clearly, doing our zazen with this in mind—and not as if we are stuck in a dark hole. Do your zazen for all of humanity; for all of those people who are not yet enlightened, sit firmly. Do not breathe in a dark hole, but burst through the entire universe with your energy, crash through the heavens with your feet at the roots of the trees, and then bring that life forth—express that life! There is nothing that needs to be forced or produced. There is nothing to think about and then bring up. Put everything into it! Do not leave anything undone and unexpressed. And then, when it is all expressed, even if kensho is not realized, how bright and fresh you will become! Zazen in a dark hole with a lot of fog will bring nothing, and you will have wasted your time. To fill up with the energy of the heavens and the earth—for that it is worth doing zazen.

The third part of Bodhidharma's Entering through Practice is craving nothing.

The various sorts of longing and attachment that people experience in their unending ignorance are regarded as craving. The wise awaken to the truth, going with the Principle rather than with conventional ideas. Peaceful at heart, with nothing to do, they change in accord with the seasons. All existence lacking substance, they desire nothing. [They know that] the goddesses of good and bad fortune always travel as a pair and that the Triple World, where you have lived so long, is like a burning house. Suffering inevitably comes with having a body—who can find peace? If you understand this fully, you quit all thoughts of other states of being, no longer crave them. A sutra says, "To crave is to suffer; to crave nothing is bliss." Thus we understand clearly that craving nothing is the true practice of the Way.

THE PATH TO BODHIDHARMA

From the birth of civilization, or going back even further, to the beginning of the earth, all these millions of years, everything has been left up to desires and instincts: liking and disliking, wanting this and that, using our bodies always for these desires, acting with anger, greed, and hate; yearning endlessly for something, always something else; always holding anger within, or always complaining about what is going on. Why are we so angry, so greedy, so ignorant? We do not even know, but there is no end to our lack of satisfaction. We are always wanting something else, something more. We are always thinking about what everybody else is doing. And for what? We do not even know. Yet even not knowing, we continue doing it—our complaining and desiring continue to arise from that craving mind.

The first of the Four Noble Truths taught by the Buddha is that we are always suffering. And why are we always suffering? Because we are always accumulating. A monk who arrives at the temple to enter the monastery has very few possessions; yet in a year he accumulates a truckload of stuff. And it is such precious stuff! We also accumulate in all of our senses: in our noses, taking in the smells of the kitchen; in the cold, wearing as many clothes as we can until we become huge lumps. We collect in our minds as well, not being satisfied with our state of mind, wanting to re-experience a past state of mind, or worrying that we are not fit for this path. Clean it all out! That is what this practice is for! Do a great cleaning of your mind!

Those who have understood the truth—those wise people who know well how the mind and society and nature and the truth work—these are the wise people. In China, a lord asked a wise man, "How can I make all of my people wise?" Rather than suggesting various activities that the lord might have his people do, the wise man simply answered, "Have them be virtuous. By thinking of others first, that virtue will gradually, naturally, become a huge expression of a sincere heart. As this expands further, peace in all the country will reign." And the old lord was very happy with this teaching from the wise man.

People of the world want everything they see. They crave it all, yet they never find satisfaction with any of it. One who has understood clearly the Buddha's teaching that nirvana exists in the extinguishing of the flames of greed, anger, and delusion—what the Buddha realized in his deep enlightenment—has obtained this same wisdom and is called an Awakened One. He or she knows this True Mind, empty and clear, containing nothing at all, without one speck. Someone who truly experiences this mind will not need one thing, not one single thing. What are you looking up in the sky and asking for, when from the origin it is all empty?

If you need nothing, then you naturally want to give away what you already have to someone else. Your enjoyment comes from giving your mind of the Dharma to everyone. Every time you come into contact with someone you give it away. People who do this are not craving, they are eager to give; that is their pleasure.

The mind of no worry, no anxiety—this is the difference between a truly ordained person and one who is ordained only in form. To worry about your life and what it will bring you is for people of the world. If a monk thinks in that way, even if he is wearing the robes of an ordained Buddhist, then he is still a person of the world and not a true monk. To be able to totally entrust, leaving everything up to the workings of the heavens— only if you do true zazen will you be able to understand this state of mind.

When we can live without great concern for our own welfare, the food we need usually comes. In doing takuhatsu, I have never had a single day of receiving no money or offering of food. If you are truly walking the path, living with only exactly what you really need, and truly practicing, you will be able to stay alive and receive what you need. It is possible to go without eating for a full month, and even if you die sitting, it will be a fine way to go. It is truly foolish, the way everybody rushes around working for the money and the food and the possessions they think they need.

At one point during my training I could not pass a koan, and was packing up my things in the monastery, ready to leave, giving up. At that time I thought it should not have taken me—or anyone else—more than three years to reach kensho. I remember my tears at the end of my first rohatsu sesshin when I could not realize kensho. Was something wrong with the way I was sitting in the zendo? I would even go out and sit all night long, but still I could not break through. So I packed my things and went to the roshi. I told him I was going to go sit for as long as I possibly could alone. The roshi asked, "Then what are you going to do?" I said I would know then, that I did not know at the moment, but when that time came I would know what I had to do. The roshi did not say anything.

I went to the Nara mountains, doing one sesshin after another on my own; I then went to different mountains in another area and did the same thing, sitting one sesshin after another. It was nearing the time of rohatsu when a young man appeared in the mountains. Neither of us had seen anyone for a few days and we were eager to talk. He asked me if I was practicing Zen, and I said, "Yes." The other young man had been doing the practice of chanting the Buddha's name, and he exclaimed, "How lucky you are, to be spending all of your time, your whole life, doing your practice!" This from someone who was able to practice only a few days a week. His words hit me like a blow on the head. At that moment, all the burdens I had been carrying around fell away, and I knew that I had never left the Buddha's palm. I became suddenly light, as if my body were weightless. I returned to Nara and found a letter from my previous training

BODHIDHARMA'S *OUTLINE OF PRACTICE*

temple asking me to come there for rohatsu.

Knowing the path would always open in front of me, I have never lost that confidence that I have never left the Buddha's palm at any time in any way. From that time on, sanzen was never terrible again. All of the koans were just my karma ripening, and to be done going on and on. Since then, the path has always been open to me. I could accept whatever came. If there was no food, it would be OK to die sitting. This is the important point: to entrust completely, to live today with one's fullest energy; to have no anxiety deep within, to have no sense of having done this or that, leaving it all up to the natural way, leaving it all up to heaven and earth.

There is a community in Shiga called Itoen, founded by a man named Nishida Tenko. He originally worked for a large company in Kobe that made woolen goods such as sweaters and blankets; he was one of the officials there. But one day he suddenly left the company, went to Hokkaido with friends, and there bought a large piece of land to farm. However, the times were bad, and the group's harvests on the land were continually poor. The others had families, and they argued about how to go about fixing things, saying they wanted such and such an amount in order to support their families, and in general could not come to any agreement about what to do with the land and the profits. At the end, Tenko was troubled, and he found the problems impossible to resolve with the other members. They eventually quit, all of them, and that ideal village was ended. They had set out to make a perfect village, and a mere six years had passed since they began. Tenko returned home penniless, with no idea of what to do next. He had no energy left to live, nor any faith left in people. He had thought that if people thought and talked about things—if they were willing to talk things out—they could make anything happen; they could have made this new village. But all his hopes had been dashed. What would he do from tomorrow? He had nobody to go home to, no money for food.

    He sat down on the porch of a shrine and thought. He thought and thought and thought. He thought all through the night, and then the dawn came and he heard a baby crying from a neighboring house. He thought, "It's crying. Why doesn't its mother get up and feed it? I wonder what she's doing?" Suddenly the crying stopped, and he knew that the baby was being fed. Then suddenly he felt as if he had received a great blow on his back; he understood something very deeply at that moment. That baby came into this world, and there was the food here for it, already. We come into this world as well, and the air, food, and water are here, provided for us—whether we think of it or not, expect it or not. This is the human source point from which we live; we are born to live, to survive.

    Tenko felt that his life was decided with that, and he borrowed cleaning tools from a nearby grandmother to clean the shrine. Later she said that her breakfast was made, and invited him to eat with her. He said he had used the shrine, and that was why he had cleaned it, but that she had no reason to feed him. She told him not to be like that, and finally he agreed to eat, for he had not eaten for a long time. He washed his dishes after eating and saw that the toilet area was also dirty. He cleaned it, and here and there as well, as he saw other things that were dirty, and finally she gave him lunch. He returned to his inn and asked if he could work there for no money at all but just to be able to live there. This is where it began. For fifty years, from that time, he never had a time of not eating. He started the community of Itoen, and all of its members cleaned everywhere: stations, public buildings, shrines. They raised gardens together and lived equally, working and laboring in a community way, giving their whole bodies, their entire energy, in service, knowing they would be provided for through that.

BODHIDHARMA'S *OUTLINE OF PRACTICE*

When we clean up and do what is necessary, what is needed always comes. Being always satisfied, looking around for where to clean next, where to straighten up next, we are able to see well and understand well where people are sad and suffering, and we have no free time for craving! This is the kind of life we must live. So says Bodhidharma.

If nothing is craved, then this world is joyful just as it is. All of it is my world, and everyone in it is my child—even the difficult and hard-to-handle children are my children. In a place called Hamanako there was a temple named Konchi, which was surrounded by rice fields spreading far into the distance. The priest was enjoying himself, commenting on what a good harvest there was going to be that year. Someone asked if all those fine rice fields belonged to the temple. The priest said, "Yes they do—we just don't receive the harvest from them." By the front gate of Sogenji we have a bank. Everyone brings money to our gate. We just don't have the bankbook for getting the money out. In the spring we have the mountains of Nara full of cherry blossoms, and in fall we have the Arashiyan River full of maple leaves. At Sogenji we have all the flowers of the mountains—we just don't pick them all. We have a huge lake with a boat in it, and it is all ours. Thinking like this we live with a great mind. It is with this kind of grand mind that we must also be doing our zazen. It is when we want to claim everything as our own personal possession that we run into trouble.

In the *Nirvana Sutra* a story is told about a man who heard a voice at the entrance of his home. When he went to see who was there, he found a beautiful woman. He was amazed at her great beauty and asked who she was. She said she was the Goddess of Good Fortune and that wherever she went wonderful things happened, that good fortune would last as long as she was there. The man was overjoyed and invited her to come in and stay for a long time in his best rooms. But soon afterward, an ugly and miserable woman came to the same entranceway. When he asked who she was, she said she was the Goddess of Bad Luck and Poverty, and she told him that wherever she went there would be ill fortune. He told her to go away immediately, but she said she could not leave because her older sister, the Goddess of Good Fortune, was there, and they always had to stay together. Greatly dismayed, the man had to ask them both to leave. Always entwined like the strands of a rope are good fortune and ill fortune. Being born we have to die; we cannot get away with only being born. We want only the good things and none of the bad. This is the life of the sentient being—wanting only the good things.

In one twenty-four-hour period we have both day and night. With both we have one complete cycle. Happiness and sadness are both parts of life that we must take together. We cannot accept just one without the other. In the *Lotus Sutra* there is a teaching about a house that is on fire—a great rich old man's house where many families lived together. All of the younger parents were out, going about their business, but the children were home playing, unaware of the great danger of fire. The old man tried to tell the children to run out, to get away quickly, but the children did not know what fire meant, nor what danger was. This story is not only about that house and those children; it is also about us, right now. How shall we spend our time? Do we have any idea when our lives will end? We know only that death has not arrived for us yet. We are still unenlightened and do not even know where we are going. Having this body we suffer. We cannot run away from that. We are planting the seeds of our own suffering all the time. Why don't we face it directly, head-on, and go beyond it!

A sutra says, "To crave is to suffer; to crave nothing is bliss." Thus *we understand clearly that craving nothing is the true practice of the Way.* Doing zazen, our bodies suffer—our legs hurt, we become sleepy. We cannot reach the place where we can forget our bodies completely. The things around us continue to bother us. "To crave is to suffer." We are all looking for something. But no matter how much we crave and receive things, we cannot take them with us; when we die we have to leave it all behind.

When Emperor Godaigo was ruling Japan, the country was divided into the northern and the southern parts, and the emperor was forced to flee his home. But he left behind a poem:

> *No matter how wonderful a wife and child*
> *and precious things—even the rank of*
> *Emperor—one has,*
> *one must leave them behind when one dies.*
> *This is just what this sutra says.*
> *How true it really is!*

This is his exclamation, that even an emperor finally has to die all alone. We think always of how we can decorate our bodies and our lives, but it is all a dream within a dream. Each one of us will have to leave it all behind eventually. Craving nothing, we realize that is the Original Mind. In that Original Mind there is not a single thing to crave. So said Bodhidharma.

The last part of Entering through Practice is the practice of accord with the Dharma.

The principle of essential purity is the Dharma. Under this principle, all form is without substance, undefilable and without attachment, neither "this" nor "that." The Vimalakirti Sutra *says, "In this Dharma, there are no living beings because it transcends the defiling [concept] of 'living beings.' In this Dharma, there is no self because it transcends the defiling [concept] of 'self.'" When the wise embrace and understand this principle, they are practicing accord with the Dharma. Since in the Dharma there is fundamen-*

THE PATH TO BODHIDHARMA

tally nothing to withhold, [the wise] practice generosity, giving their bodies, lives, and possessions without any regret in their minds. Fully understanding the emptiness of giver, gift, and recipient, they do not fall into bias or attachment. Ridding themselves of all defilements, they aid in the liberation of living beings without grasping at appearances. In this way they benefit themselves and others both, gracing the Way of Enlightenment. In the same fashion, they practice the other five perfections. To eliminate false thinking in practicing the six perfections means having no thought of practicing them. This is practicing in accord with the Dharma.

Though this is the fourth and last part, it is in fact the most important. In Christianity we have, from the beginning, God. But in Buddhism we do not put the Buddha first. We have the Buddha, the truth he preached, and those who follow it, but that truth—the Dharma—comes first. On the eighth of December, under the bodhi tree, the Buddha saw the morning star and realized his True Mind, exclaiming, "That's it! That's it! That's me shining!" Having spent six years doing severe training, getting rid of everything, in that deep samadhi he realized that new life out of a place of complete emptiness. What was the substance there? That body of nothingness, seeing the trees and hearing the birds—what is that? What is that which is clearminded, that which is beyond expression?

Believing that he could not make anyone understand, he thought about keeping this experience to himself, since no one would believe him anyway. But it is said that when he returned to his deep samadhi, the gods came to him and told him he must share this experience and guide others to it through expedient means. Probably there were no gods actually talking to him, but rather a difficult inner struggle as he tried to figure out how to communicate an experience that was beyond words to the rest of the world. He at last knew that he had to teach this to all others; he had to teach his deeply spiritual fellow Indians. They already honored many gods and prayed to mountains and trees, since everyone wants something to believe in and to worship. But the Buddha knew from his own experience that even if there were many gods, there was not even one to be prayed to. There was nothing as wonderful, as sublime, as that very mind which he had now realized. This was the Dharma, the source of all life, of the sun, the moon, the flowers, and all the Ten Thousand Things. This was the source of life consciousness, the roots of Mu. This is what we have given the borrowed name of our True Mind. This clear, bright mind is all that exists, and it itself gives birth to all those gods. This mind that the Buddha had newly realized—this deep life within each of us—was given the name of Dharma.

The Buddha brought forth the Four Noble Truths, the Eightfold Path, the Twelve Ways of Causation, and went to teach of his experience to his five training friends, who all attained enlightenment on the spot after hearing what he said. These were the first *sangha* members. At just that time there came a rich young man who had used up all of his money and was now broke. He was going to the mountains to commit suicide when he met the Buddha. The Buddha told him of his realization, and the young man attained enlightenment on the spot and became his next disciple. Then the rich young man's father came looking for him. He, too, heard of the Buddha's realization and became enlightened himself, and was the first to call him Buddha, the Awakened One.

The Buddha taught in a way that could be applied to anyone, but it was all explanation that had to break through explanation. He taught that it was necessary first to realize the true source—not with conceptualizations, but by actually knowing for oneself the genuine essence—or it would be nothing more than interpretation. The Dharma in its essence is pure. It is above defilement and attachments; it cannot be soiled, it cannot be decorated; it does not increase, it does not decrease; it has been here from the origin and it cannot die. Consciousness can die, but its source, its roots, do not. That which gives birth to consciousness does not die. There is never too much nor not enough. In every single case the source is just as it is, never soiled or clean. It is sometimes called the universe, but that is already an imagined thing, an explanation.

Shakyamuni said, when he gave the flower to Makakasho, "I have the True Dharma Eye, the Marvelous Mind of Nirvana, the True Form of the Formless, the Subtle Dharma Gate, which does not set up words and phrases, and is a separate transmission outside the scriptures. This I entrust to you Makakasho." I have found mind, that place where nothing gets stuck, he was saying, not that place of no thinking, not that place of saying when we walk that we are not walking, of saying when we sit that we are not sitting, but the place where we are not stuck on the thought of those things, that place of just becoming that sitting, of just becoming the life energy of whatever we are doing, of whatever comes to us.

The True Dharma Eye, the source of all that is: This is what the Buddha passed on to his disciples, who continued passing it on to their disciples, to Bodhidharma, who passed it on to Niso Eka. But what *was* transmitted? When people see someone point a finger at the moon, they always look at the finger, when the point of course is to see the beautiful moon. The "moon" we must see is that understanding that was passed on by each person to another who became pure by realizing that source of all, the true root. To know the Dharma, our True Nature, to experience that same thing which the Buddha experienced—to understand each other—we have to experience this for ourselves. It cannot be found in thinking about it or in reading a sutra or in trying to understand it with our heads.

When the Buddha was about to die, Makakasho asked,

BODHIDHARMA'S *OUTLINE OF PRACTICE*

"To whom shall we turn to guide us when you are gone?" The Buddha replied, "Take refuge in the Dharma. Find guiding light in your own true, pure mind. Never look outside yourselves for it. Even if there seems to be something wonderful outside yourself, that will only lead to confusion and doubt." If his disciples had not themselves attained enlightenment as well, they would not have been able to understand. If they had only read about it or heard about it, their experience would not have been the real thing.

Through twenty-five hundred years of history, this life energy has continued, filling up the eyes of those who could see. They all could see with those eyes of the Buddha; they could see the whole world clearly. We, too, can experience it like that. When asked, "Why did Bodhidharma come from the west?" Joshu answered, "The oak tree in the garden." Simply that oak tree, right in front of his eyes. That was it. Joshu was deeply enlightened, completely selfless, egoless, and true when he said this. It did not have to be an oak tree; it could have been anything. It could have been the mountains; it could have been the rivers; it could have been a different kind of tree; it could have been a stone. What is right in front of your eyes? Are you becoming one with it? Is your state of mind such that there is not a stain left? Cut through to the core, vast and wide—this was Joshu's state of mind when he said, "The oak tree in the garden."

We open our eyes, we open our ears, we feel sensations in our bodies and minds, but isn't it always the past that we are looking at? Yesterday's menu? What is it that is right here in front of us, right now, completely new? It comes to us, touches us in our whole body, fresh and alive. What is it? Are you feeling this, knowing this as your own experience? If you are tasting this, then you know Joshu's state of mind well. He is not stuck in feelings, thoughts, and ideas. He is one with society, one with the whole world; he is not stuck inside himself, but right there, completely filling up the heavens and the earth. We must promise ourselves that we, too, will understand it like this.

Our True Nature is pure; this is the Dharma; this is what Bodhidharma is teaching us here. In our basic humanity there is no color, no space, no time. It is empty from the origin. As Rinzai puts it, "In this lump of red flesh there is a True Person of No Rank always coming in and going out. If you have not seen it yet, see it now! See it now!" This True Person of No Rank is neither woman nor man, neither rich nor poor, neither clever nor foolish, neither adult nor child, nor does it have color or shape—and yet, from our eyes it becomes mountains, rivers, birds, and the oak tree in the garden. From our ears it becomes the song of the birds, the sound of the wind—all the sounds of the Ten Thousand Things. From our nose it becomes the fragrance of the flowers and all the smells of the Ten Thousand Things. With our body we feel heat, cold, pain, and all the other sensations possible—this Person of No Rank, always coming and going freely! If you have not noticed it yet, even while using it yourself, at this very moment meet it, right now! We are urged in this way by Rinzai.

This life force is neither good nor bad, nor is it stained by the outer world. We are usually stained by likes and dislikes, becoming attached to things that bring us joy and trying to avoid what we dislike. But because our very center is pure and unstained, there is truly nothing to be attached to! In truth, there is no such being as a sentient being, because everything is a part of the basic True Nature. In the Dharma, in our purest self, there is no ego, because we are not attached to a small self. Those who have realized the truth, who have understood it with their own experience, have the same understanding as the Buddha because the mind that is understood is the same mind, without any attachment, moving freely. To live in this way is to practice the Dharma. One who has understood deeply will always be living in this way easily.

If you live in this essence of the Dharma there is an unchanging center that has no wish to possess. It can be truly sad when meeting a sad person, and be ready to do whatever is possible for a suffering or miserable person, helping not just physically but with the totality of one's life energy. The closest thing to this completely selfless functioning may be the love of a mother for her child. It can be called instinct, yet it is more than that. It is possible to call it the purest human emotion, yet it is not limited to humans; it is found in animals as well. Practicing charity, giving offerings, never being greedy with property, body, or life—this greatness of mind is found in one who truly loves humankind with a pure, clear mind. It is one expression of the understanding of True Mind.

We become greedy because our ego appears; we become begrudging and unwilling to give. Shudatsu Chooja, a very rich man in old India, was said to have had hundreds of warehouses full of gold and silver and other possessions. But he was a truly generous man, always following the Buddha's teachings and giving everything away. Whenever he saw a poor person, he would immediately give him or her things. Everyone around him respected him greatly. But this giving had its limits, and possessions have their limits as well, and one day his warehouses were empty. He had to let all of his servants go, and only he and his wife were left. They spent days without enough to eat. During this time, Mokurin Sonja was sent to their home by the Buddha for takuhatsu. Shudatsu Chooja's wife had just sold their last wooden box and had bought only enough rice to last for the next few days. Yet when she saw Mokurin Sonja coming on takuhatsu, she gave him almost all of her rice, feeling very good about what she had done. But then after him came the Buddha. So she gave him the rest of the rice. To give when you have is easy; to give when you do not have is much more difficult. When the woman's husband came home and found no rice he cried out in dismay until he heard the details of what had happened. Then he told her that she had done her best in giving all of the rice, and he said, "Let us go look for something that might have been left in the warehouses or somewhere." But the doors of the warehouses would not open. They tried one after another until finally one gave, and looking inside they found the warehouses to be again full of gold and silver. This is of course a symbol of spiritual wealth.

Ikkyu Sojun, a Japanese Zen master of the Rinzai school, was out one day, being given dinner. Because he could not eat all of the food he was offered, the lady of the house gave him what was left to take home. On his way home he met a beggar, and feeling good and full of food he gave the beggar the box of food he was carrying. The beggar received it and said nothing. But Ikkyu said to the beggar, "Don't you think you could at least say 'Thank you'?" Again the beggar said nothing at first; then after a while he replied, "Yes, but you feel better than that for giving something, don't you?" To be thankful that we can give something is the natural expression of our True Nature.

Through takuhatsu—one of the most important practices left by the Buddha—we learn of this threefold nature of emptiness, this emptiness that is the essence of Dharma. The giving, the receiving, and the things given: all are one and all are emptiness. Once we realize this emptiness, whether what is given is $10,000 or $10, it is all the same thing. Those who are giving, and those who are being given to, must give and take with no prejudice, no egoistic attachment. In India, the monks went out in the early morning, without making prostrations or offering any other expressions of thanks. They were served the first rice in the pot by the people they visited, although they came for the leftovers. To receive and give with an empty mind, with no ego attachment rising, is the point of this practice of takuhatsu. It

BODHIDHARMA'S *OUTLINE OF PRACTICE*

teaches us the threefold nature of emptiness and enables us to rid ourselves of attachment to the things we receive and give. In Japan, people bow to each other and consider that a practice to cut the conceited ego. The most important point, however, is not to be attached to any form whatsoever; this is the most important lesson.

The practice of charity, just as it is, saves society and aids in the development of the Buddha world. The other virtues—such as endurance, meditation, great care, and wisdom—are also for the purpose of saving society and ourselves, and all of them originate from within our own True Nature. The way of the mind is to endure but not get angry. As we do zazen, by enduring the pain, the cold, and the wish to move around, we develop and express our True Mind, the source of all activities. To want to clean and care for everything around us, to help those in trouble or those in need—these are activities of our True Nature; they are nothing but the expression of our Original Mind, just as it is. To move when we should move and yet be totally still when we are still, expressing appropriately the love for humanity that comes from our deepest mind—to be able to do this is to practice the Dharma.

But what is most important is to function in this way without being aware of it. The same is true for each of the practices Bodhidharma has listed—the practice of requiting animosity, the practice of accepting circumstances, the practice of craving nothing, and the practice of accord with the Dharma. For them to arise naturally and of themselves is of the greatest importance. This is the world that Bodhidharma is writing about in his text. That source of what is listening, right this minute; of what is seeing, right this minute—no matter who you ask or what you read you will not find the answer in words. You must experience this eternal life, your Original Nature, for yourself! Each of you please realize these roots, and from this foundation, standing firmly on that realization and experiencing it thoroughly, reveal that life beyond explanation—this place of no time and no space, that which is from the origin empty. To experience this True Nature is what we must all do! And for the doing of this, we have zazen.

Zazen

JOSHU JUSHIN WAS BORN in China during the Tang dynasty (618–907). A student of Master Nansen, he attained enlightenment at the age of eighteen and continued his training with Nansen until the latter's death nearly forty years later. At the age of sixty, after several years of tending his teacher's grave, Joshu left on a pilgrimage, vowing, "I will ask even a child of seven to teach me if his understanding is greater than mine, and I will teach even a man of one hundred if my understanding is greater than his." For the next twenty years he traveled to every corner of China, seeking out teachers and studying the Dharma until, at the age of eighty, he was invited to the city of Joshu to become abbot of the temple Kannon-in. There, until his death at the age of 120, Joshu devoted himself to instructing the many disciples who gathered around him. Among Zen people he is regarded as a model of ideal Zen practice and living, and is noted for his penetrating use of words—"Joshu's lips," it was said, "flash light."

One day a monk came to see Joshu. "I'm a new monk who has just arrived. Please teach me what is important in training—how should I live my life?" The monk was undoubtedly hoping for a few precious words of guidance to treasure and follow in his Zen practice.

Joshu, however, responded from precisely the opposite direction. "Have you eaten your gruel this morning?" he asked. The monk was probably surprised by Joshu's seemingly irrelevant response—he had requested instruction on how to go about Zen training; he did not expect to be asked if he had had his breakfast. Joshu, however, was not asking just about the monk's morning meal. He was pointing to a central aspect of training: the need to be attentive in whatever one does. When the monk answered, "Yes, Master, I have eaten," Joshu immediately responded, "Then be sure to wash your bowls!" With this the monk suddenly understood what Joshu had been saying.

This story tells it all. The words *zazen* and *training* are constantly on our lips, and we never tire of talking about Dharma and Truth, making it seem as though there is something special and out-of-the-ordinary to be attained. This only proves that our true creativity has yet to come alive. We may have reached a certain understanding on the level of reasoning and logic, but we have still to see the very place upon which we stand; we may have fathomed the workings of the universe, but we have yet to grasp the essence of our very own minds.

People often ask me if zazen can ever be of any practical use in these complex and turbulent times. By way of answering, let us consider the concept of *aligning*. The word *align* signifies the idea of situating everything in its proper position relative to everything else. First we align our body, then we align our breathing, then we align our mind. And once these things are accomplished, we find that we cannot be satisfied with aligning only our limited individual minds, but that we must finally align ourselves with the Mind of the larger Self that pervades all existence.

Since the process of alignment starts with the body, let us begin with the physical side of Zen practice. There are four aspects to this physical side, corresponding to the four basic postures—*gyo*, "moving"; *ju*, "standing"; *za*, "sitting"; and *ga*, "lying"—that a human being assumes during the course of the day. There are times in which we are engaged in activity (*gyo*), during which we attempt to remain focused and aware; times of standing still (*ju*), during which we attempt to return to the source and observe the content of our minds; times of sitting (*za*), during which we delve even deeper into our inner source; and, finally, times of lying down (*ga*), when we rest our bodies.

The first of the four postures, "moving," is fundamentally not one in which we turn inward and observe ourselves—activity requires that we direct our energies outward toward whatever it is we are doing. Standing still permits a greater inner focus, but it is in the posture of sitting that this element finds its deepest expression.

I once heard a raconteur of the traditional Japanese comic anecdotes known as *rakugo* say something about the relation of sitting and comedy. Genuine humor, he commented, touches upon something universal in human beings, something that cuts across individual and cultural differences. If this universal element is missed, even the most skillfully related rakugo will fail to evoke either laughter or sadness in the audience, even if the people see the story's point. The raconteur then added that it is extremely hard to move people at this deep inner level when they are standing, but relatively easy when they are sitting, particularly when they are sitting not in chairs but solidly on the floor in the traditional Japanese fashion.

Thus there is something about the sitting posture that facilitates access to the deeper regions of the heart, and this is as true of zazen as it is of rakugo. When we assume the sitting position we quite naturally draw closer to something universal in the human spirit. Merely sitting is not in itself sufficient to bring about peace of mind, of course, but it does have a certain settling effect on even the most troubled soul. This is something we experience at a far more fundamental level than that of intellectual speculation. Doctrinal questions—for example, "What is salvation?" and "What did the Buddha teach?"—are certainly important, but in zazen it is more essential first to find that state of settled tranquillity in which all of humanity has a share.

Differences in culture, language, and national temperament definitely exist, but there is a certain "place" of settled tranquillity where we all naturally come to rest.

Zazen is not a matter of intellection; it must be rooted in the physical sense of inner liberation that is most easily experienced through sitting. This sense of liberation is not in itself enough, however. It is also necessary to attain an inner state open to the essential nature of things. If liberation was all that mattered, it would be enough to drug ourselves to sleep, but this would hardly resolve the problem of how to act in our everyday lives from a stable inner essence, regardless of how turbulent or dangerous the outer circumstances are. It is here that the importance of sitting emerges, for it is through sitting that we are most easily able to stabilize ourselves in this inner essence.

Thus, although we can say that moving is Zen and sitting is Zen, it is important that we first master the basics of sitting meditation so that we may best experience this inner essence. There are three central aspects of zazen: the aspect of body, the aspect of breathing, and the aspect of mind.

The bodily aspect concerns the physical posture of zazen. In meditation, the aspect of mind is in many ways central, but the body-mind relation is such that unless attention is paid to the details of proper posture, it is extremely difficult to achieve anything on the mental level of true zazen. Sitting for even a thousand years with a slack posture will leave you just as confused and deluded as ever.

The body may be considered in terms of the section above the waist and the section below the waist, and both have their respective roles to play in the overall balance of zazen. The upper portion must be light and relaxed, while the lower portion must be firm, taut, and settled. We might compare the physical form of zazen to that of a pyramid, broad and stable at the base and gradually tapering toward the top, until it reaches a single point. The folding of the legs during meditation into the lotus position puts one in firm contact with the ground, creating a calm, stable foundation for both body and mind. Either full lotus or half lotus is fine, though the full lotus is preferable since the half lotus more easily results in a loss of balance and consequent injury to the legs.

The folded legs comprise a triangle where the knees form the two base angles and the coccyx forms the apex. The buttocks are pushed back and the lower abdomen is pressed forward, while the trunk rises perpendicularly from the middle of this foundation, forming a balanced centerline for the overall body pyramid. The lower back is curved in as much as possible to provide a solid support for the upper trunk; sitting with your back bent out may seem more comfortable, but it easily leads to sleepiness and random thoughts, and it makes the attainment of deeper meditative states impossible. The upper body should rise up in a light and relaxed manner, almost as if it is not there. The chin should be pulled back and the top of the head thrust upward, while the neck should touch against the back of the collar. With the body in this posture the strength will quite naturally settle into the *tanden*, the place in the lower abdomen, two or three inches below the navel, that forms the physical and mental foundation of zazen practice. It is important, however, to think of the tanden not as a specific point on the body but as something that appears when a number of factors are in proper balance—the tanden is, in a sense, the expression of an overall condition. It will not appear unless the upper trunk is relaxed, the back is straight, and the lumbar area is firmly tucked in. When the back is curved in as far as possible, the trunk naturally straightens and the *ki*, the vital energy, flows freely upward along the spine.

The use of zazen cushions, known as *zafu*, makes it easier to maintain this posture. Do not sit right in the middle of the zafu, since this tends to shift the body's centerline backward, rendering it harder to sit properly and defeating the cushion's purpose. Instead, place yourself more toward the front of the zafu, so that the body slants slightly forward and the back curves naturally in, easing the burden on the lumbar muscles. Make sure the cushion is of the appropriate height—people with years of experience may be able to sit well even with a relatively low cushion, but beginners usually need to raise the pelvis higher to aid the proper in-curving of the lower back.

When you start a period of meditation, particularly if you are a beginner, straighten your spine by leaning forward slightly, then leave your pelvis tipped forward and your lower back curved in as you bring the rest of your trunk to an upright position. Continue to rock forward and backward until you find the proper point of centeredness. Doing this will provide a quite clear sense of both the lower back and the tanden. Some practitioners find themselves sleepy, unfocused, or full of scattered thoughts nearly every time they sit. I've found that almost always this is because their back is not curved in and their centerline is off.

Whether sitting in full lotus or in half lotus, it is easiest to maintain your balance if you pull your feet up on your thighs as close as possible to your trunk; it is when you sit with your legs not high enough that they become numb and painful. The soles of your feet should face upward and not out to the sides. Attention to such details of posture is very important in finding the right physical alignment. Of course, your legs will hurt if you remain in this position twelve hours a day, but you need not make an endurance contest out of zazen. Try to sit in this manner, focused and straight, for even just a single short period every day.

When sitting, it is important to close your anal sphincter muscles slightly, as this helps keep the lower trunk in the proper position and in the right state of tautness, promoting the free flow of ki up through your tanden and backbone to the top of your head. When this flow is present, the back straightens naturally and the entire body comes into proper balance with the centerline. When the body is thus properly aligned—the lower portion taut and firm, the ki flowing freely, and the upper trunk straight, light, and relaxed—the mind, too, becomes settled, and extraneous thoughts are minimized. In contrast, when you sit in a careless fashion, inattentive to the details of posture, your ki, which should flow freely throughout your system, stagnates in the upper regions. This makes it difficult to bring the body into proper balance and causes painful stiffness in the shoulders and neck. The stability of the lower trunk is thus disturbed, causing a loss of balance in the entire body; you feel unsettled and over-react emotionally. Even the ordinary activities of daily life become difficult.

In this way, the study of Zen must proceed through the body—theorizing alone cannot lead to the inner experience of true zazen, in which your ki fills your tanden and provides a sense of boundless energy that seems to extend to the very ends of the universe. When you are grounded in your physical center and the various bodily parts are settled in their proper positions, the energy circulates naturally; the spine is straight, and the entire physical structure rests in a position of optimal balance, like a pagoda rising up with each story settled firmly on the one below. By maintaining this posture not only during zazen but in daily life—in walking, in working, and in all other activities—you remain centered in your lower abdomen, so your upper body feels fresh and light and you are filled with a sense of clarity.

This will be aided by loose clothing that does not restrict the flow of your breath. Another factor to be careful about is eating. Meat and other greasy fare thicken the blood and should be reduced; the emphasis should be on good nourishment. The matter of sleep, too, is important—neither too much nor too little is good for zazen.

One receives energy and support from food, from sleep, and from the surrounding environment. A balanced approach to these factors not only helps your practice but also contributes to good health, and a state of good health is, needless to say, the most suitable physical condition for the practice of Zen. I might add that it is best to sit with other Zen practitioners, so that everyone can sense everyone else's zazen energy and draw strength from their efforts to harmonize the mind. It works the other way around, too—it is quite difficult to sit among people who have no interest in meditation.

One's inner, mental environment is also important. You must make a conscious decision to practice, vowing from deep within to bring your body into balance, to harmonize your breathing, and to clarify your mind. Merely crossing your legs and sitting vacantly on a cushion is not enough. Unless you express your commitment in the form of conscious, directed effort, you will never be capable of genuine zazen.

It is very important also to keep your eyes open during meditation. Sitting with closed eyes may seem a good way to cut off distractions and achieve a state of inner silence, but doing so usually encourages drowsiness and extraneous thoughts. Even if you succeed in reaching a tranquil state of mind, this is nothing but hothouse Zen, of little use to you amid the challenges of everyday life. Furthermore, the senses, particularly sight and hearing, provide the most basic link between the outside world and the activities of the mind. Unless we learn to integrate such sensory input with our zazen, our training will be of little practical use.

Let us now move on to the matter of aligning the breath. Settled, well-regulated breathing is basic to Zen practice and is vital to the realization of the inner essence of zazen. When the breath is disturbed, it is impossible to observe things accurately and make appropriate judgments. Moreover, shortness of breath often leads to shortness of temper—one loses one's sense of perspective and reacts solely on the basis of the immediate circumstances. You become overly affected by what people say and are easily swayed by the events around you, leading to further disturbance and delusion. All of this signals that your breathing is not in order. Regulating the respiration means maintaining your breath in a relaxed and unobstructed flow regardless of the situation you find yourself in.

Begin your zazen with *shinkokyu*, "deep breathing." The kind of deep breathing practiced during athletic warm-up exercises generally focuses on inhalation, but in zazen it is the exhalation that is central. It might be called "exhalation-type deep breathing." This necessitates, first of all, that the upper body be straight and completely free of tension. Centering your respiration in your tanden, begin with an exhalation; if you start with an inhalation there is a tendency for the body to stiffen. Exhale completely, using the mouth, not the nose, for the first several breaths. After this, breathe through the nostrils. The respiration should be neither overly forceful nor overly gentle—it should feel full and expansive, as though it extends infinitely and without constraint. The breath should feel as though it comes not from the chest but directly from the lower abdomen, as though there were an open pipe directly connecting the tanden and the mouth.

Do not force the breath, but allow it to flow completely out in a relaxed, expansive way. If the upper body is completely free of tension, the settling of the strength into the tanden area will occur in a quite natural way. Continue the exhalation for about thirty seconds or more if possible, breathing out every last bit of air until the abdomen becomes convex. At the very end of the exhalation some tension tends to set in, so try making two or three light, gentle pushes—this heightens the sense of the tanden and makes the transition to inhalation quite natural. When the in-breath is complete (generally it does not take long), begin the next exhalation, again letting out all the air until the abdomen is concave and finishing in the same manner with two or three small pushes.

This type of breathing, in which the air is released until the belly becomes concave, is called abdominal breathing. Try to take about ten breaths in this way, being careful to exhale fully with each one. When the exhalation is complete, the ideas filling the head are, as it were, expelled along with the air. This is the best way to effect the mental "turnabout" that enables you to leave behind the agitations of everyday life and begin zazen with a mind that is fresh, clear, and empty. With only a partial exhalation, your mental state in zazen remains a mere continuation of what was in your mind before.

When you have settled into this abdominal breathing, with the shoulders and chest free of tension, the entire upper body relaxed, and your strength seated in the tanden, then a shift takes place—from abdominal breathing to tanden breathing. In the former, the abdominal muscles play the major role in the drawing in and letting out of the breath, expanding and contracting to enable long, relaxed, free respiration. This quickly brings about a settling of ki in the tanden, which in turn gives rise to a sense of strength and stability in the area between the lower back and the lower abdomen, drawing the consciousness there and filling it with relaxed energy. In this state, the abdomen remains rounded and nearly motionless even as the breath moves freely in and out, as though (in the words of Hakuin) there were a fully inflated ball inside. Were the belly to be poked from the outside, it would feel taut and firm but not rigid.

Once this tanden breathing is mastered, you can maintain the zazen state of mind whether you stand or sit, work or talk—in the words of Yoka Gengaku's *Song of Enlightenment*, "Walking is Zen, sitting too is Zen; speaking or silent, moving or still, the essence is undisturbed." This is not easy at first, of course, and we soon become scattered as we go about the activities and interactions of daily life, but as tanden breathing matures, you will notice how your inner state remains the same in all conditions, even during sleep. This is because in tanden breathing, the body and the respiration have come into a state of oneness; it is not something performed through willpower, but something that the body does quite naturally. For the same reason, the body is always relaxed during this type of respiration— it is only when the conscious mind tries to influence the breath that tension and stiffness set in.

    This state of integration alone, however, is not in itself enough to bring about the third type of alignment mentioned above: alignment of the mind. Attaining the stability of a well-aligned mind is essential in Zen training, since most of us do not live in a quiet world of our own, cut off from other people, but are instead surrounded by the constant distractions and demands of everyday life. In daily life there are, of course, important matters that demand careful thought, but so much of what fills our heads is utterly unnecessary. We constantly replay emotionally charged situations and fret endlessly over personal relationships, overloading our minds with thoughts that are of no real account. One memory leads to another to create an endless chain of ideas that clouds our awareness and confuses our mental functions. We end up unable to judge situations accurately and therefore act in inappropriate ways.

    In Zen, it is through the practice of susokkan or the koan that alignment of the mind is attained. Susokkan, which literally means "counting-the-breath meditation," is the most basic practice in Zen for mind-alignment. It is not a mere breathing exercise, as it is often regarded even by experienced Zen practitioners; rather, it is the primary means by which we gather the ki in the tanden, and it leads to a thorough cleansing of the very roots of the mind. Traditionally, susokkan is said to consist of six "wonderful gates"—that is, six aspects or stages. The first is called *su* (literally, "to count"), in which one counts as one observes the inhalations and exhalations; the second is *zui* ("to follow"), in which one comes into harmony with the breathing and simply follows its movement as it flows in and out; the third is *shi* ("to stop"), in which the mind is focused in a state of oneness; the fourth is *kan* ("to observe"), in which one sees clearly and directly into the true nature of all existence; the fifth is *gen* ("to return"), in which the all-seeing eyes attained at the *kan* stage are turned inward to see clearly within oneself; and the sixth is *jo* ("to purify"), in which one reaches the state where not so much as a speck remains.

In susokkan, the out-breath should be long and steady. One breath after the other, inhale and exhale with the entire body, keeping centered in your lower abdomen and taking care not to force the outbreath, as this would prevent the expansive, free respiration necessary to zazen. The full exhalation should last for ten to fifteen seconds (or, for beginners, for about eight seconds, with eight seconds for inhalation, so that there are about four complete breath cycles a minute). As you become accustomed to this type of breathing, the exhalations will grow longer, while the inhalations will remain about the same length.

As mentioned above, the first stage of susokkan is counting the breaths; the counting in and of itself is not essential, but in the beginning it helps focus the attention on the breathing process. Slowly and expansively become one with each number, breathing and counting in a relaxed, unhurried manner free of all tension. Generally, one counts in a series of from one to ten, but it is also possible to count from one to

ZAZEN

a hundred or from one to a thousand, or even just to recite "one" over and over again. Allow the exhalations to be full and complete, aiding the process with the two small, relaxed pushes described above—this will lead to a very comfortable breathing cycle.

Again, the respiration in susokkan must not be forced or artificially controlled, as this would simply constrict the breathing process. Do not count in an automatic manner, but with relaxed yet complete attention. You must apply yourself unceasingly and with single-minded sincerity to this careful counting, working with ever-fresh attention and creativity. Exhale from the lower abdomen in an open, relaxed manner until your belly feels totally empty and the in-breath begins spontaneously; if you are too hasty or hurried, your practice will become mechanical and your mind will remain restless and unable to deepen into a state of intense concentration. At the beginning, your trunk tends to pull backward and the movement of the abdomen feels unnatural; you become very self-conscious about how the process is going, and about whether you are "succeeding" or not. As your sitting ripens with constant practice, you will be able to remain with your breathing quite naturally, your body in perfect harmony with the rhythm of respiration.

Focus on each individual breath, one after another, centering your consciousness in your tanden and filling it with energy. Breathe each breath totally, then forget it and move on to the next. Superficial concentration is useless—you must feel that the respiration is piercing through the ground to the very ends of the universe. Let no gaps appear between your concentration on one breath and the next. Continue like this, one focused breath cutting off all thought of the one before, cutting and cutting and cutting until there is no room for random ideas, no room for concepts of self, no room for inner noise. Your body, the zendo, the entire universe are all contained in this total focus on the breath, in this utter singleness of mind. There remains nothing to hold on to, nothing to depend upon.

This condition is known as samadhi of susokkan, where only the breathing and the counting remain; one has become the breathing; the mind is occupied with nothing else. In this state of true emptiness you feel completely refreshed, full of energy, and taut, yet fresh and lucid. This is the state of the first "wonderful gate" of susokkan, that of *su*.

In this way, follow the coming in and going out of your breath from morning until night. Count and count and keep on counting the breaths whether you are doing zazen or not; count whether you are standing or sitting, whether you are asleep or awake. As you continue, the inhalations and exhalations become completely natural, and finally you enter a clear, open state of perfect unity between mind and respiration, where it is no longer necessary to count to help focus your attention. This stage, in which the awareness and the breathing are one, with no need for numbers, is that of *zui*, "following."

Then, at a certain point, all awareness disappears. This is the stage of *shi*, "stopping." When this will happen cannot be predicted—it must occur naturally; it cannot be produced or forced. Some time after this "stopping" takes place you come back once again to awareness. This is *kan*, "to see." Again, you cannot deliberately generate this state, it must happen of itself. Following this is *gen*, where you forget yourself completely, and finally *jo*, a state of mind that is bright, clear, and transparent. In all six of these stages—the natural path to samadhi—it is vitally important that one not attempt to force things but simply allow the process to unfold on its own.

Although six stages may be identified in the practice of susokkan, it is the first two—counting and following—that are most important. Once these are experienced the rest will follow of themselves. Do not get caught up in analyzing your progress or attempting to determine which of the six stages have been attained—just stay with the breathing. You must become the breathing. This is the most important point. The nature of the respiration varies, of course, sometimes becoming deeper and sometimes becoming shallower depending on whether you are working, reciting sutras, or sitting zazen, but press on until you can no longer tell whether it is you who is breathing or the breathing that is breathing itself.

This state must be deepened to the point that all connection with the outside world is cut off and nothing whatsoever touches or enters your awareness. This does not mean, however, that the senses are shut down. Externally, the correct way to cut off connections is to collect the mind into a single point and maintain this state of absolute attention and clear awareness. Internally, it is to avoid holding on to anything at all. Do not get caught by thoughts or fantasies—just let the breath flow in and out while staying with susokkan or your koan. Allow the images that arise to come and go as they will—like pictures passing on a screen—but keep your awareness focused on the breath, allowing nothing to linger in your mind, until you and your breath become one.

Breathing never stops—it is with you all the time. You need only remain attentive to its flow. Even if thoughts arise, even if stimuli press in from the outside, just push on without pause, allowing no breaks in your awareness. Put everything into the process and move relentlessly ahead. No matter what comes along, do not let it become an obstacle. If you lack the courage to advance in one continuous line, you should not begin in the first place. To do zazen and susokkan just because you think you ought to will never lead to a true understanding of the mind. If you want to touch the True Mind that connects each and every one of us, you must be willing to push beyond any problems that arise.

Bodhidharma likened such perseverance to the stability of a wall: "Cutting away all connections to external things, letting go of all concerns within, when our mind is like a firm, tall wall we are then at one with the Way." But the idea is not to be hard and stiff. Whether sitting, standing, or engaged in the activities of everyday life, just maintain your awareness of the breath. If you proceed in this way, the noisy, bothersome thoughts that fill the mind will eventually quiet down, and all the ideas you once thought necessary will fade away. With all the stimulation in today's world, this does not happen easily, but if you continue with a straightforward effort you will eventually realize a state of mind that is full and replete, a state of mind so still and clear that, like the depths of the ocean, neither wind nor wave can touch it.

Koan work and susokkan are not about attaining a quietistic state; they must become your total life energy, engaged in with the entire body and with the inner eye fully open. The first case of the *Mumonkan* explains it clearly: Zazen must involve every bit of your mind and every bit of your being, all "three hundred and sixty bones and joints and eighty-four thousand hair follicles." In the face of such total awareness, random thoughts and fantasies soon vanish. In true zazen, not so much as a speck must remain of dualistic notions of self. Our existence fills the universe, and it is this existence that speaks words, that moves the body, that carries on the activities of everyday life. It is only when we realize this inner essence that koan work has any meaning. Zazen is not a trance—the eyes are fully open, the ears are fully open, the mind is fully open, the inner and outer worlds are one. It doesn't matter if you are sitting in the zendo, walking, or cleaning the grounds; the essence is the same.

In this way align your mind so that absolutely nothing superfluous remains. This is the state called "no-mind," the nature of which is impossible to explain; thus we describe it as

ZAZEN

"a fully aligned mind." The spirit should always be clear, vast, and luminous. Not that we should cling to the notion of maintaining an empty mind or endlessly tell ourselves to avoid all thought—this is still delusion, and must be transcended as well. Nor, of course, should we go about searching for understanding in books or the words of others—this simply causes uncertainty and aimless wandering of the mind, quickly dissipating any concentration that may have been gathered through zazen. When filled with thoughts, the mind tends toward anxiety and dejection; when free of them, it becomes naturally fresh and relaxed; our facial expression clears, and our lives are filled with light. From this is born the true way of being and living.

This explanation, however, does not yet express the full purpose of zazen. At the entrance of a Zen temple we often see the words *kyakka shoko*: "Watch your step!" What these words are telling us is to be aware of everything we do. We take off our footwear attentively and in such a way that later no one has to rearrange it correctly for us. We put our shoes at the side of the entranceway, not in the middle, so that other people may more easily slip out of their shoes. In this way, even to the way in which we take off our shoes, continual awareness is necessary.

The words *kyakka shoko* do not, of course, apply only to our feet and shoes. They remind us to remain attentive in our entire way of living. If we keep our room in order then our home is kept in order, and next our neighborhood is kept in order, and next society is put in order. In this way, step by step, the nation, the natural environment, and finally the whole planet are put in order. The entire universe then comes into order. Thus, when we regulate our own mind, this circle extends to include the whole planet, and then the entire universe. To align your own mind, to put it in order, is to correct and put society in order.

When Master Joshu said, "When you've finished your gruel, be sure to wash your bowls!" he was showing us how the process of creating order is not something special or unusual. It is living a simple and natural life in a simple and natural way. If we do this, then order manifests naturally and of itself—there is nothing special that has to be done in order to produce or maintain it. In your everyday life, if your way of being is in order and your mind's creative and inventive energies are full and consistent, then everything around you will spontaneously and naturally come into order as well. This is living zazen, useful throughout our lives.

When the Buddha spoke from the top of Vulture Peak, he held a single flower in front of everyone. This was not just any flower—it was the Buddha's experience, the manifesting of the Buddha's very essence. Even if it is true that humans are simply another type of animal, as some people so dismissively put it, we are not here simply to live out our lives eating and sleeping. If we simply live and die as the animals do, then our existence as human beings has no significance. To be truly human we must live in a humane and dignified way. We are not alive merely to accumulate things and fulfill our desires. Our life, our mind— how brightly can they shine and illuminate all that we encounter? Zen is the direct realization of the divine light as it exists right here within our bodies. To have the exquisite teachings of the sutras come forth from our very own bodies, expressed in our every word and every action—that is the point. Unless we experience this our Zen is not genuine. With our wonderful human mind and spirit we are not mere animals; we are called to live our lives in the best way possible. This is the understanding that Master Joshu expressed so that the young monk, too, might be able to understand.

If we view our zazen as something separate and independent from our actual, everyday lives, then it has no meaning whatsoever. In this real world, in our actual living bodies, we must discover to what degree we can refine and develop our creative and inventive potential, and to what extent we can shine forth with a great and brilliant light throughout our lives. We must examine ourselves always in this manner, employing the same creative energy we use in our zazen to see ourselves clearly and never turn our gaze away. To develop such watchfulness to its highest level is our most important task.

It is through zazen that we nurture and develop this ability. Thus we can see the crucial importance of meditation in the insecure, ever-changing society of today. Zazen enables us to live in a way that expresses our true humanity, so that we can live and develop in accord with the truth.

One lifetime is not so very long. In the time you have left, live in the way indicated by Master Joshu when he said, "When you've finished your gruel, be sure to wash your bowls!" How brightly can you make your bowls shine? You have to work energetically and deeply on this! It is not someone else's problem—only you can resolve it. Your life in this world is not someone else's responsibility, it is your responsibility. To grasp this deeply is what Zen teaches us. If one person truly understands, then that person's way of living will have a lasting effect on all of society.

Hakuin and His *Song of Zazen*

ALL SENTIENT BEINGS *are essentially Buddhas.*
As with water and ice, there is no ice without water; apart from sentient beings, there are no Buddhas.
Not knowing how close the truth is, we seek it far away—what a pity! We are like one who in the midst of water cries out desperately in thirst. We are like the son of a rich man who wandered away among the poor.
The reason we transmigrate through the Six Realms is because we are lost in the darkness of ignorance. Going further and further astray in the darkness, how can we ever be free from birth-and-death?
As for the Mahayana practice of zazen, there are no words to praise it fully.
The Six Paramitas, such as giving, maintaining the precepts, and various other good deeds like invoking the Buddha's name, repentance, and spiritual training, all finally return to the practice of zazen.
Even those who have sat zazen only once will see all karma erased. Nowhere will they find evil paths, and the Pure Land will not be far away.
If we listen even once with open heart to this truth, then praise it and gladly embrace it, how much more so then, if on reflecting within ourselves we directly realize Self-nature, giving proof to the truth that Self-nature is no-nature. We will have gone far beyond idle speculation.
The gate of the oneness of cause and effect is thereby opened, and not-two, not-three, straight ahead runs the Way.

THE PATH TO BODHIDHARMA

Realizing the form of no-form as form, whether going or returning we cannot be any place else.
Realizing the thought of no-thought as thought, whether singing or dancing, we are the voice of the Dharma.
How vast and wide the unobstructed sky of samadhi!
How bright and clear the perfect moonlight of the Fourfold Wisdom!
At this moment what more need we seek? As the eternal tranquillity of Truth reveals itself to us, this very place is the Land of Lotuses and this very body is the body of the Buddha.

For those of us who make zazen our primary practice, these words of Hakuin Zenji in the *Song of Zazen* are of great importance. They are an excellent guide for understanding the actual essence of doing zazen. Before we look at the *Song of Zazen* itself, however, I would like to tell you about Hakuin Zenji. This will help you to understand. Hakuin Zenji is one of the greatest figures of Japanese Buddhism. Today, the Zen Masters who transmit the Dharma in the Rinzai line are all descendants of Hakuin Zenji. The lines of Zen that flowed from the Kamakura and Motomachi eras down to today all joined in Hakuin Zen to become Japanese Zen. Although Hakuin Zenji has also been criticized in various writings, his enormous influence continues to the modern era. As one ancient put it: "There are two things of Suruga that are great beyond anything else, the great mountain of Fuji and Hakuin of Hara." The people thought of Hakuin in this way even when he was alive; he was famous and well loved and deeply respected.

For information about Hakuin's life, we have the records of Torei Enji, one of his top disciples. We know that Hakuin Zenji was born in 1685 in Shizuoka Prefecture in Numazu at Hara, at the base of Mount Fuji. At the age of four, he was already expressing great brilliance and genius. At the age of seven, he heard a Dharma talk on the *Lotus Sutra* at a temple and memorized the entire sutra by heart. At the age of eleven, he was taken by his mother to a talk at a temple where he heard about the terrifying horrors of hell for the first time. He was so deeply frightened that he began shaking and trembling. Perhaps more than most children, he was very sensitive and nervous. He wept and grabbed at his mother's knees, weeping and crying. "Hell is too scary! Hell is so scary! Even when I have you nearby, hell is so scary! If I fall into hell it will be terrible! Please make it so that I do not have to fall into hell!" He was a child very affected by things. At the age of twelve, he heard a monk say, "Even if in fire, it won't burn, even if in water, it won't drown." Hearing this, he made a vow and gathered his own mind to realize this state of mind. He imitated the monk by taking a fire tong that was heated to red-hot and touching it to his calf, to try to see if he, too, could do this without being burned. This is how dedicated he was.

It has been said that Hakuin was a man who lived his life while he kept an eye on hell. As a young man, he carried his fear of hell with him, and it was perhaps as a result of that fear that he yearned to be ordained. At the age of fifteen, overcoming his parents' reluctance to his being ordained, he became a monk with their permission. He was ordained at Shoinji in Hara by Tanrei Soden. This priest ordained and supported him and gave him the name Ekaku. When Hakuin was seventeen, Tanrei died; under another teacher, at the age of nineteen, he began actual training.

One day, when reading the records of the old Chinese masters, Hakuin found the account of Ganto Zenkatsu, a famous Zen master who lived during the Tang dynasty. When Hakuin read that Ganto had been killed by bandits who cut off his head, he was stopped short. His deep fear of hell had sent him into training. He had become ordained to be liberated from that great fear, and now he learned that a great master who had already completed his training had been slain by thieves! He had been sure that a person who did such training would have enough merit to change evil thieves into good and faithful people—that there should be enough Dharma power in a man like Ganto to accomplish something like that. Was Ganto no different from an ordinary person in society? Hakuin thought that if Ganto's death was in spite of all that training, then the training must have no meaning whatsoever.

Just as huge as his hope and expectation had been, so was his disappointment and discouragement. "Everything was the bragging left by the old masters—nothing more—fantastic stories with nothing real in them." With these thoughts his training lost its vitality. He had no motivation and he suffered. For many months, he would not sit or study. He wrote poems and read books, doing whatever he felt like. Still, he remained unsettled. His mind was insecure, hopeless, and tired; every day he was in deep despair. What had that all been about? For what had he been training? How should he live now? He could find no answers.

One sunny day at the temple where he was living, the monks were airing the old books to rid them of bugs that might destroy them. Facing all the books sitting there, Hakuin made a vow and put his future in the hands of the gods: "Please tell me in which direction I should go!" he prayed. "Please, I promise that I will follow whatever you tell me to do!" From the bottom of his heart, Hakuin Zenji made this deep commitment. Then, from the pile of books spread all over the room, he took one in his hands and opened it.

The book he happened to pick up was by Jimyo Insui. In the old days, this splendid teacher, Jimyo, told about going to the temple of Funyo Zensho Zenji. Funyo Zenji was a very, very strict and outlandish teacher who would not let just anyone come into his temple to train. If you became even the slightest bit drowsy, Funyo would beat you and tell you that you had to leave. So, as Jimyo sat outside Funyo's temple hoping for admittance, doing his full and taut zazen, he held an awl just above his leg so that if he started to fall asleep the point of the awl on his leg would awaken him. He worked diligently and creatively on his practice. People of old always said, "Great efforts will, without exception, bring great Realization. To be alive in this world without any reason or result—to live and yet be known by no one—for what are we born into this world if this is how it is?" Jimyo kept himself going with these thoughts, making extreme efforts with intensity, and he was finally allowed to enter Funyo Zenji's dojo. In later years, the Dharma of that same Funyo Zenji, of whom all people and beings were frightened, was transmitted to Jimyo. Hakuin, reading about this, thought that if you do not believe deeply enough in the Buddhadharma—even if you think about why these people did what they did for training—it must be because you have not done enough yet, and he corrected his thinking. Over and over again he would say to himself, "Great efforts bring great Realization." Again and again and again he gathered his courage and once more began training.

At the age of twenty, having decided how the rest of his life would be lived, Hakuin Zenji traveled to the east and to the west looking for teachers and places to train. At a temple in the Banshu area he wrote this poem:

The mountain's flowing waters surge forth the
Buddha's sermon endlessly.
If you would practice in the same way that these rivers flow,
before long you will without fail realize kensho.

THE PATH TO BODHIDHARMA

He did zazen at this temple, which was located at the top of a mountain. From the mountain, he could hear the flowing waters of a river in the valley below him. Listening all night to the sounds of the river as it ceaselessly made its way to the sea, he knew that if a person made a firm commitment and deep vow to practice in this same unceasing manner, if a person could continue in this way without stopping, then that person's realization was guaranteed. One would awaken to the True Mind without mistake. He then trained with no books or brushes or calligraphies or pictures or inkstones—none of it at all. He pursued his path with total determination.

In the spring of his twenty-fourth year, Hakuin was at Eiganji Temple in Takata, in the Echigo area. At this time his training was well advanced and his state of mind had ripened to the place of no inside or outside—to where it could not be known what was himself and what was Mu. He was truly still and clear—truly serene. His was the state of mind of the mute person who has seen a dream and cannot express it, that of sitting without knowing you are sitting and standing without knowing you are standing, of speaking without even knowing you are speaking—the world had become like one smooth layer of Muji, completely closed into this one layer. This was that moment just before one's own purified mind extends throughout the heavens and earth. People of old said that great efforts will without fail produce great light! Hakuin vowed deeply in his mind and began a sesshin sitting in the graveyard. He began his sitting determined not to stand again until he had attained enlightenment. He continued intensely with this determination and entered a great samadhi. At dawn on the last day of this sesshin, from far away in the dim light of the dawn, he heard the sound of the temple bell. At that moment Hakuin Ekaku Zenji jumped up and cried out, "That ringing! That ringing! That is me ringing! That is me ringing!"

HAKUIN AND HIS *SONG OF ZAZEN*

His still and clear mind had been pierced through by the bell's sound, and that and every moment was full of deep wonder. Great joy filled every movement of his hands and feet. Hakuin expressed it jubilantly: "Ganto has never died! He is here, right here. Alive, just like this!"

He had struggled for so long and had endured so much, and finally all of those efforts were coming to fruition. He felt that no one had had such a deep experience for at least three hundred years. He was in such deep wonder that he became very excited. And when he saw people everywhere suffering, he was moved to tears that the Buddhadharma had come to this earth to help them. He was deeply, deeply moved. Yet the priest of Eiganji, Shotetsu, could not do anything with him. Hakuin had fallen into a severe case of conceited self-importance. This Hakuin Zenji, if he had stopped there, would never have become as famous throughout the world as he is today. The great functioning that he expressed in his life would never have been possible.

The person who was responsible for bringing about this turnaround was Dokyo Etan Zenji, familiarly known as Shoju Rojin. The person who encouraged Hakuin to see and speak with Shoju Rojin was Doju Sokaku, his only disciple.

When Hakuin arrived at Shoju Rojin's hermitage, the teacher questioned him immediately, "How did you see Muji?"

"Muji! There is no place to lay a hand on it."

Shoju Rojin immediately took Hakuin's nose in his hand and twisted it, saying, "You say it can't be touched, but this is how much it can be touched!" He became furious with Hakuin, and Hakuin saw the extent of his conceit and dropped it immediately in front of Shoju Rojin. He became like a baby with him. Next, Shoju Rojin asked him how he had seen the koan of "Where did Nansen go when he died?" "How about it: Where did he go?"

No matter what Hakuin answered, Shoju Rojin would not accept it. One time Shoju Rojin grabbed him and hit him and almost threw him off the porch—this was how strong and energetic he was. He yelled at Hakuin, "You stupid priest—stuck in the dark hole and blind besides!" Hakuin had experienced that Mind of the Great Death, but from there he was unable to function; he was stuck and fixed. With that reborn consciousness and way of being, he was deeply troubled. Whenever he encountered Shoju Rojin, Shoju Rojin would call him "that Ekaku Joza who is stuck in a deep dark hole." It is written that Shoju Rojin would hit him and pull him around. Yet Hakuin Zenji stayed with Shoju Rojin and trained at his hermitage for eight months.

One day Hakuin was doing takuhatsu in the town of Iiyama. Still working on the koan about where Nansen had gone when he died, Hakuin was standing in front of a house steeped deeply in samadhi when an old lady came out of the house and told him to go to the other side of the street. Because he was in deep samadhi, he did not hear her. The old lady became very angry. "If you don't get over there across the street, I will hit you with my broom!" She began hitting him, and he suddenly came to and spontaneously encountered his true Life Source—that actual Truth was touched. Koans that he could not have touched before he could now pass one right after the next. He saw them all in one flash. He was so full of joy, he returned to see Shoju Rojin. When Shoju Rojin saw how Hakuin looked, he confirmed his experience completely.

But while Shoju Rojin confirmed Hakuin's experience, he did not confirm his understanding. Leaving Shoju Rojin's hermitage, Hakuin returned to Numazu to nurse his former teacher. While there he continued to deepen his practice, but his body was so tired and exhausted from his great efforts that he became depressed and sick with tuberculosis. He became so sick that even the most famous traditional doctors of the time gave up all hope of saving him. He then went to visit a hermit, Hakuyu, who lived in the deep hills near Shirakawa in Kyoto. From this hermit he was able to learn the hermit's method of staying healthy and healing—the *naikan*, the healing practice of introspection. With this method his sickness was cured. He saw that it might be easy for any person of practice to have this same kind of experience, to lose the meaning of practice, to become conceptual, and so he wrote a book, *Yasen kanna*, in the common language that would be easy for anyone to read and understand.

After the age of twenty-eight Hakuin continued to deepen his understanding by going on pilgrimages to meet the great masters in Fukui, Aichi, Mino, and elsewhere. Here and there he looked for the masters and did his inventive practice, steeped in samadhi wherever he was. At thirty-two, he finally returned to the temple where he had been ordained, Shoinji. He taught the many disciples who came to him and worked in society a little bit at a time, giving life to his experiences through Dharma talks. At the age of forty-two, he once again took in hand the *Lotus Sutra*, which he had not looked at for such a long time. As he read the section entitled "The Chapter of Examples," he coincidentally heard the sound of a cricket crying weakly underneath the porch and was suddenly awakened to the deepest truth of the *Lotus Sutra*. At the age of sixteen he had thrown down this sutra, declaring it simpleminded; now, twenty-six years later, he was finally able to realize its truth.

In his diary he described how, without even thinking about it, he had given a great cry of joy and astonishment. He must have been deeply moved. Until then he had thought this sutra was a shallow work without much meaning, and he had taught people in this way. He realized now that he must apologize from the roots of his being for having done this. At this time, also for the first time, he understood what a great state of mind Shoju Rojin lived in every single day of his life.

THE PATH TO BODHIDHARMA

Shakyamuni Sesson, the Buddha, had not deceived people after all! This he also understood: In Buddhism there is only one straight path—this fundamental truth of the Mahayana he now understood clearly. He was now able to live the Buddhadharma freely. As the Buddha had put it, "Everywhere in these three worlds is my home and all of its beings are my children." This great compassion of the Buddha was absorbed more and more deeply into his being. He knew without doubt that all beings are from the origin Buddhas, and that all of these Buddhas have come into this world to open the eye of wisdom in all beings—to open and enlighten this eye of wisdom. In all of its subtlety, he saw that there is nothing but this in the Buddhadharma. The exemplary teachings in the *Lotus Sutra* were to illustrate this and teach how to do it, like a mother trying somehow to get her child to be able to understand. In teaching how to understand the mind of humans, this sutra expresses the compassionate mind and wisdom of the parent who first chews the food in order that the child will be able to eat it. Hakuin realized this great kindness he had not understood before, that great determination of the Buddha to liberate all beings, to leave out not even a single one. The immensity of this all-embracing, compassionate mind was what he could then also feel, and in his deep and intense amazement he could not hold back his overflowing tears. At the beginning, when he had heard about being in fire without being burned and being in water without being drowned, looking for dreamy miracles, he had become ordained. But now he knew that that which he had finally realized, that great, all-embracing compassion of the Buddha, was his very own life energy as well.

In the *Lotus Sutra* it is written, "I do not have any feeling against you, nor deride you. You are one who will become a Buddha." In this way it is said to both old and young people, to both rich and poor people: prostrate and realize this vow.

HAKUIN AND HIS *SONG OF ZAZEN*

Shakyamuni's mind is expressed in this teaching clearly. For those of us who do zazen, it is in the realizing of this that we are able to be rid of our own heaviness. To awaken to this, we let go of the layers of accumulation and realize the essence. This is what our zazen teaches us. For all beings to be liberated it is required that all beings be awakened to this very fact.

From that time on, Hakuin Zenji worked with truly sharp intensity. In his fifties and sixties, never resting and not needing to regret the passing of a single wasted moment, he taught the many disciples who came to him, spoke wherever he was invited, did calligraphy, painted, and wrote, leaving simple texts and dynamically working in every direction.

At the age of seventy-nine he was a little sick, yet he never rested. On New Year's Day in the year 1768, he said, "I will this year be eighty-three—an old monk—but I have never had such a wonderful New Year's. It is so wonderful and I give great thanks!"

That year—in December of 1768—he was sick and was visited by the local doctor. The doctor took his pulse and concluded that there was nothing to be concerned with. Hakuin said to the doctor, "If you cannot recognize that a man is going to be dead in three days you must really be a blind quack!" On the tenth of December, Hakuin called his disciple Suio and told him how he wanted things to be done from then on. On the morning of the eleventh of December, quietly laying on his side, Hakuin gave a great growling sound and died. Six years later he was given the posthumous name of Jinki Zumyo Zenji, and following that he was also given the name Shoju Kokushi.

Hakuin Zenji's *Song of Zazen* begins, "All sentient beings are essentially Buddhas." Religion is the seeking of the eternal, the perfect, the pure, and the absolute good. To put it another way, we can say that it is the seeking of God or Buddha. Is this God or Buddha inside us or outside us? We leave that question for now, since there are different ways of looking at this depending on the fundamental point of view of various religions and practices. Yet all religions seek this eternal purity and perfection. There is no difference in this. This is why religion is necessary—because we are not perfect and pure and because our life is not eternal. Because we are incomplete we seek something in God or Buddha to complete this imperfect, small self.

In the records of Buddhism we read that the Buddha at his birth immediately stood and walked seven and one-half steps. Pointing his right hand to the sky and his left hand to the earth, he said, "In all the heavens and on earth only One is holy." This may be only a legend, but it holds the flavor of Buddhism in a kernel. It tells us that our own mind is our place of refuge. His walking seven and one-half steps is about the freedom and rights of humans as they walk on the earth. He did not say "In all the heavens and on earth only One is holy" in order to say how superior he was. He was not saying it to call everyone but himself a fool. As the representative of all humans he was saying that the human being is the most splendid of all creations of heaven and earth. He was saying that humans are free. There is nothing that can deprive us of our true freedom and actual rights. If we return to our Original Mind we will always know that place of absolute dignity and profound meaning. In each being there is this true clear mind. In Buddhism—in its basic teaching—we have this point made clearly: Humans are free and dignified. This wisdom and deep compassion are encompassed by each one of us, and this absolute freedom cannot be denied. If we think of it in this way, we can see how this legend of the birth of the Buddha has deep meaning for the teaching of Buddhism.

The Buddha was born a prince. He was versed in all the philosophies and schools of learning taught in India at that time. In the martial arts, he was able to throw off all challengers. He had a summer palace and a winter palace—and autumn and spring palaces as well. He was this rich and this full of blessings, and not missing anything in his pleasant life. So why, then, did he leave his beautiful wife and adorable child?

He left his deeply respected father, against his father's wishes. He gave up all of his possessions and political power and left his countrymen. Why? He had seen how meaningless material and animal pleasures are, and he had seen that no matter how we try, it is impossible to fully and completely satisfy the urge for them. He had understood this melancholy state of mind thoroughly. He went to the mountains to find true eternal life and meaning, to know true joy. He sought the answers there to his questions and a resolution to the unfulfilled path he had been walking. He was taking on the greatest problems of all beings and making a determined commitment to resolve them. Someone had to do it, or the truth would never be realized.

For six years he continued his ascetic training. At the age of thirty-five, on the eighth of December, near the bank of the Nirenzen River, near Bodhgaya, he glanced at the morning star and was suddenly and deeply awakened to the Supreme Truth. At that moment, without even thinking of it, he said, "How wondrous! How wondrous! All beings, without exception, are endowed from the origin with the same bright, clear mind to which I have just been awakened!" That is to say, there is in the deep mind of each person a clear, pure, and eternal state. This true place is what he was enlightened to. It is not external to us. This was the first declaration, since the beginning of humans, of the true liberation of all beings.

In his *Song of Zazen*, Hakuin Zenji is telling of this great wisdom—this compassionate wisdom that we all have from the origin. This resolution is expressed in the first line: "All sentient beings are essentially Buddhas." Beginning with this conclusion he commences his *Song*. He puts that most basic teaching of Buddhism in his first line, teaching us about zazen. By putting the conclusion first, he shows us the basic tenet of Buddhism that relates to all beings: Why, when we are born into this world, do we suffer and become deluded and confused? The answer is expressed in the next lines. Many ways of liberating ourselves from delusion are spoken of, but the Mahayana teaching is the most important. In accordance with the teaching of samadhi as the way of utmost importance, we are able to encounter that true quality of our Original Mind, and finally, "this very body is the body of the Buddha" is known clearly. This is the overall flow of this *Song of Zazen*.

Even though it says in the very first line that "All sentient beings are essentially Buddhas," we are all born with both a very thick egoistic layer as well as the clear mind of Buddha. Yet the next line tells us that this egoistic layer and this clear, purified mind of Buddha are in fact the very same thing. We may perceive them as separate, but they are in fact only two sides of the whole: "As with water and ice, there is no ice without water; apart from sentient beings, there are no Buddhas." An old song says that rain, snow, ice, and hail are no different from water; when they fall they all become the same water of the valley's stream. Water becomes rain, becomes snow, becomes sleet, becomes hail, becomes ice, becomes frost. The form changes, but the source material is one and the same. Ice and water are of the same material and essence, but they are completely different in shape. Water is warm; ice is cold. Water has no form; ice has a form. Water flows; ice cannot flow. Water seeps into any place and leaves no cracks between itself and its container; ice cannot blend or accommodate. Water can bring life to trees and plants; ice harms trees and plants and kills fish. Water and ice are of the same material, yet because their form is different they function differently. They are very different, yet they are in essence the same. In this same way, Buddhas and ignorant beings are different yet also the same.

HAKUIN AND HIS *SONG OF ZAZEN*

The water that gives life can also be destructive. Sometimes there are great floods, and in these great floods homes and precious belongings are destroyed. A piece of ice is hard and resistant, yet if you heat it, or if it is touched by the warmth of the sun, it melts and turns to water. "As with water and ice, there is no ice without water." As there is no ice apart from this water, our chunk of being egoistic is also part of our clear Buddha Nature. Even that mind which is concerned all day long with winning and losing and gaining and profiting, even that mind, just as it is, is the mind of the Buddha. There is nothing separate or different from that.

For ice to become water, heat must be applied. For human beings to return to the Original Mind, they have to throw away everything and offer themselves to society; they must let go of all delusive and extraneous thoughts. The only question that actually exists is: Do we have the wisdom to make use of that mind? We learn to prosper, to bring ourselves what we need, to take care of ourselves, but do we have the wisdom to work not only for our own good but also for the good of all beings, of all people in society, of everyone in the world? This wisdom knows that our greatest joy is the growth and prospering of all people, not for the good of our own selves but because when everyone grows, everyone flourishes, and we flourish as well.

Yet if we are not careful, that small egoistic view immediately pops up again. And we are once more caught up in our own self-centered concerns, once again we are working only for our own comfort, taking care only of our own small, limited, narrow needs. Because we are not satisfied with this way of being, we look outside ourselves—we read books, we go to hear somebody talk, and we think about things external to ourselves instead of looking within. We look everywhere outside ourselves seeking some explanation, some reason, some excuse. "Not knowing how close the truth is, we seek it far away—what a pity!"

THE PATH TO BODHIDHARMA

Usually, those people who enter the path of Zen have already read too many books and have done too much thinking about Zen. They want somehow to actualize all of the complicated explanations and all of the words they have picked up from those books. What they are attempting to do is truly a difficult thing. In fact, for zazen—which literally means "sitting Zen"—it is better not to read so much but simply to sit, as the word implies. What sits is not our mind but our body—that is the base.

In the olden days people would study and then, to understand what those studies did not reach, they would do zazen. To do zazen is to realize that place study does not reach, the true realization that cannot be experienced through scholarship. What is the actual source point of every human's nature—the original body of the universe?

We deal with this deep and vast question through zazen because it cannot be understood with our heads. That which can be explained can be found in books. This path, however, has to be experienced. Although there are many books about Zen, it is better to keep our heads empty. We need to let go of all knowledge or information and awaken to that with which we are already endowed at birth—this is zazen. What has to be done is not to learn something but to awaken to something—this is zazen. We have to let go of intellectual studies, of any idea of how much we already know, of how many books we have read; then we have to just sit. To deeply awaken to that Original Mind is what we do in zazen. That which is the base of doing this is our body. That is why it is necessary to correctly align our body and to awaken to our clear pure nature and the natural wisdom that springs forth from within us. The natural sense of how things truly are will become clear to us from within. From the bottom up we have to look once more at everything and see life as a whole, not in small separated parts. This is Zen. The body is always the base. The actuality of this is what we have to align—this is zazen.

If we speak about zazen in this way, people will assume they understand right away and think that it is enough just to sit, that all the teachings in the world are beside the point, that we must not be entangled in confusing words. To just sit and think nothing—we imagine what this is, and think we should turn our backs on society and go into the mountains and do this and only this. If we choose not to go to the mountains, we still do the same thing by trying to maintain silence in our mind. We mistakenly think that this is zazen. And this kind of thinking is a very common mistake. If we were to just sit and separate ourselves from everything, would we be resolving our challenges, would we be bringing forth our true and correct inner wisdom?

Can we learn to read what is in nature, to let nature teach us its wisdom? Can we truly find that wisdom within ourselves? We are all full of ideas and thoughts and information and past experiences and dualism, yet our internal essence separated from all that is the True Source of everything. By returning to that mind, we can learn true wisdom from those true ways of thinking and seeing. As long as we are caught by our own narrow point of view and our attachments, we cannot see with this true wisdom. Even if we have the true teachings of the ancients, we can see and learn only from our own small self-centered point of view. We have to let go of our thoughts completely and read the clear wisdom of the ancients and learn from them. The Buddha was the first great teacher who realized this true wisdom, but many other great saints have realized this during the twenty-five hundred years since. We take Zen, handed down from them, as our place of refuge. Through Zen we look for truth and see things correctly—for doing this, before anything else, we learn the teachings of the Buddha.

THE PATH TO BODHIDHARMA

These teachings of the Buddha—this same wisdom transmitted by the many teachers who have passed the Dharma teaching down from one generation to the next—have guided many people on the path. The Buddha's first great teaching was that life is suffering. We must see this directly. Everyone likes to be happy. Yet even while living in happiness we must not let go of the truth of life: that there is great suffering everywhere. To see the source of this suffering is what is of the next greatest importance. Next, we have to look at this suffering correctly; if we do this we will, without fail, be liberated from such suffering. We are taught to believe deeply that each one of us can be liberated and then live as an awakened person. For this we enter the path and thoroughly clarify it to its ultimate point—this is how liberation works. This is how the Buddha taught his disciples. This teaching can be found in the *Flower Garland Sutra* or the *Lotus Sutra*, earlier sutras in which these teachings are frequently repeated. The words of the Buddha, as we look at them quietly and carefully, sentence by sentence, need to be realized not with our heads but within our daily lives. If we give them life and practice, then our minds will be freed from their delusion and confusion.

We become simple and clear, and from within ourselves our minds become liberated. This process is one of understanding not with our heads but with our bodies. We need to do it in our daily lives; whether we are sitting, standing, or walking, we need to keep doing it as if in one straight line. When we can hold just one word—looking at it and concentrating on it all the time—the clutter in our minds will be swept away naturally, and our minds will become truly vast and luminous. Our Bodhisattva vow to awaken everyone to this truth will become full, and our desires will no longer catch us in attachment.

The Buddha's disciple Shuri Hanroku is an example of this. He was a very foolish person, not very intelligent at all. The

HAKUIN AND *HIS SONG OF ZAZEN*

Buddha said to him, "Get rid of the clutter, sweep your mind clean," and Shuri Hanroku actually took up a broom and a rag and cleaned all day, every day, to keep this process ongoing. He then had an exemplary awakening to that deep wisdom no different from the awakening of the Buddha. Without any scholastic ability, and even with a terrible memory, if we do that which we have received as teaching with every ounce of our being, every bit of the time, our mind will of its own become liberated. This is very mysterious, it has to be said.

The words spoken by the Buddha feel very far away as the days and centuries go by, and we need more intimate and familiar words to guide us. Zen is taught within the living air of every era; it must function in a way that is alive, vivid, and full of essence. From China there is the famous Mu koan of Joshu. Other koan lines are the answer to the question of why Bodhidharma came to China, "The oak tree in the garden," or Master Unmon's answer, "Every day is a good day."

These short phrases became themes and questions to be understood—not by using your head but by sitting quietly and concentrating only on this until, without even knowing it, these words become your state of mind, a state of mind that is no different from that of Joshu or Unmon. These koans are united in all people of training and touch the true source of each person's mind. What is important is to sit and concentrate on one thing until you become that state of mind of no thinking. Then everything you have learned externally—knowledge, past experiences, dualistic awareness—will fade away. You will separate from them and return to that state of mind in which you were born, and the original true wisdom will come forth. Your mind will shine, vast and luminous, with this wisdom's light. You will be able to experience life from a place free of attachments and see it clearly, exactly as it is.

To be able correctly and truly to see with this eye of wisdom is the most important thing, and that is what we are given the ability to understand. This way of seeing allows us to give to all people an acceptance of life just as it is. This state of mind of acceptance is what is naturally born from this seeing.

We have to separate ourselves from our ego filter and the idea of self on which we are stuck. It is true that there is also the small "I" that lives, but we cannot function from the essential way of being and the true way of seeing when we are stuck and attached and unclear. The small self is always obstructive to the higher quality way of doing things. Those who find the higher way of doing things are the ones who do Zen and work hard to let go of their small selves. People who do *kendo* and are obstructed by their small selves are unable to know their opponent's mind. If they cannot see the other's mind, their movements become small and limited; they cannot move in a large and free-flowing way. For those who do flower arranging, if the arrangement is full of their own small-minded concepts, then the flowers will be full of a sense of self-importance, and there will not be any true harmony. In tea ceremony as well, if you present tea with dualistic ideas coming first, then the tea will not be served freely and without the stain of small-mindedness. There is no smooth flow to it, and while it is perhaps harmonious in form, it is not harmony from the deep heart. In the Noh theater or in calligraphy or in archery, zazen is given life in this same way. After we have learned the technique we can go beyond it and separate from it, becoming one with the entire universe. In this way, we can give life to a magnanimous functioning.

Likewise, in martial arts, we cannot be always stuck on winning and losing; we have to crush that attachment, and for doing that we have zazen. The sixth successor in the Dharma from Bodhidharma was Rokuso Eno, who said of zazen, "To not allow any mind moments of concern with what is happening outside of us, this is *za*. To look within and not be moved at all is *zen*." This is his definition of zazen. Our awareness can move inward and then also outward. To be where there is no concern with any of the phenomena in the world—good and bad, beautiful and ugly, deluded or enlightened, sin or salvation, gain or loss—is za. To look within to where the awareness arises and to see its essence, and in seeing this to awaken to the source of this awareness—not being deluded by anything or moved around—is zen. This is the sixth patriarch's very practical way of putting it. In fact, zazen, or za, is not to sit and say we cannot think, that we should not think. Rather, za is the place where we have lost track of all of this. Zen is not saying, "You cannot let that mind move, you should not move your mind around to this and that!" It is not struggling like that. But when your mind is well aligned, it does not go wandering around. This mind that does not stray from the Original Nature—this is Zen. This is how the sixth patriarch defined it.

We sit and become clear, free of obstructive thoughts and fear. This is the very important essence of Zen, but it does not mean that we should become like a rock or a tree. We must not make this mistake. "Never abiding in any place yet manifesting continually." When the sixth patriarch heard these words from the *Diamond Sutra*, he became deeply enlightened. We cannot say that the mind is empty and then try to guard that state of conceptualized emptiness. True emptiness does not arise from a preconceived notion of nothing at all. It is what comes forth when the mind holds on to nothing, when in each moment and in each situation we can function freely. Yet we do not move and change independently and individually; we do not act pointlessly and without meaning. That is very important. We have to look at nature: It never tries to prove and push itself; only humans do this. Nature is just as it is, changing in accordance with the seasons. In springtime, the flowers blossom; in the summer, the leaves become full and green, and the trees make fruit; and in the fall the leaves return to the ground to begin the preparation for the next year's cycle. Animals as well live in accord with nature, not as if one being is more important than another. This is true for all beings in existence; nature always moves toward the newer, greater existence.

Life should not to be regarded in the narrow sense of birth and death. Rather, we must know the bountiful flow of the life energy of the whole universe. This is the way nature is. Only humans hold on to attachments, and we sink into likes and dislikes. These are very high levels of emotion, but there is a difference between holding them important and drowning in them. When we drown in them everything becomes suffering. Instead, we must live every single day anew, every day fresh again. In each second every new moment is born anew. Confidently and firmly living each moment—this is the human's natural way of being. When laughing, laugh from your deepest heart; when crying, cry from your deepest heart; when it is necessary to be angry, be angry from your deepest heart; and in this way you can fill the heavens and the earth with the essence of what you are feeling and then leave nothing behind. With a full and abundant mind we live in this original state of mind, in the way of the healthy mind. To experience this essence is zazen. This place of no attachment, this free state of mind, is zazen.

Experiencing the Original Mind directly and teaching others to do so as well—that is what the lineage of Bodhidharma is guided by. We have his guiding words: "To see the clear mind directly and become a Buddha." There are other ways of teaching it, but this is the direct way. By directly perceiving that mind which holds on to nothing whatsoever, immediately and at this very moment, each and every person can awaken.

Kyogen Chikan Zenji died in 898. In his younger years, Kyogen Zenji trained with Hyakujo Ekai Zenji. When Hyakujo

Zenji died, Kyogen continued sanzen with his older brother disciple, Isan Reiyu. When he was in sanzen, the priest said to him, "When you were with Hyakujo Zenji, it was said that when given one you would answer with ten. You have a reputation for being very clever, and you are said to have read everything that has been written on Zen. Still, I am not interested in hearing what you have read or learned or heard from someone else. What is it that you knew before you came out of your mother's womb? Before you knew any words—say one word of this!" This was a very tough problem! Kyogen certainly tried very hard and said many things.

"Mu."

Isan replied, "But that is what Joshu said."

"Form does not differ from emptiness."

Isan responded, "But that is what is written in the *Heart Sutra*."

"From the origin there is only one bit of emptiness."

"But that was already said by the sixth patriarch."

No matter what Kyogen said, Isan Reiyu told him that it was all someone else's words. That face before you were born—prior to any experience and learned knowledge—what is that? Speak it from yourself. So Kyogen reread everything and all of his notes on everything as well. Still, Isan would not accept anything he offered, only calling his answers the fart gas of the ancients—no matter what Kyogen tried it all got him nowhere. When finally he had nothing else to say, Kyogen pleaded with Isan to show some compassion and tell him the answer. But Isan just laughed and said, "I want to tell you, but then it will be with my words. You have to speak your own answer with your own words."

Kyogen had studied so hard, and now he could not speak even a single word. How pitiful! It had all come to nothing. He felt he had no potential and would never be able to go back to society, so he decided to go and take care of the cleaning of a cemetery and not to show his face to anyone. The successor of the sixth patriarch, Echu Kokushi, was buried in a secluded place in the mountains, and this is where Kyogen went.

Kyogen spent his days cleaning that cemetery on the mountain. Still, in his mind, there remained the question Isan had asked him: Give one word from before you came out of your mother's womb. These words never left him; all day long they rolled around inside him. He became desperate in his contemplation. One day, when he went to the bamboo grove to throw away the leaves he had raked, as he did every day, a piece of tile hidden among the leaves hit the bamboo and made a loud clunk! On hearing that sound Kyogen was deeply enlightened. "This is it! This sound! I did not hear it from anyone, nor did I read it in a book! This sound is what was received by that self before I was born—that is it!" He felt it directly, so joyfully it came up from the very bottom of his mind. He looked far into the distance, in the direction where Isan was, and lit incense and said: "Isan, great priest! You did well to chide me so thoroughly! If you had not kept me going like this, I would never have tasted this flavor today." Kyogen had been able to go beyond that place of preconceived notions and ideas, forgetting time completely, forgetting even his own existence, and from there he heard that sound, clunk! At that point his consciousness was directly perceived as well, that which came from nowhere at all; in this pure awareness was his face before his parents were even born, his True Self. To say it another way, it was life as it is, not the physical body, but that life energy which fills the heavens and the earth— this is what he experienced. This is enlightenment, *satori*, and when we know this experience, the things we see every day are fresh, and each day our mind is new.

What we have to do is to separate ourselves from that

dualistic awareness and knowledge that we have accumulated since birth, to go beyond that and to cut through its root completely. We have to realize our True Nature without giving any attention to those thoughts and deluded ideas. When we have encountered Original Mind, then we know that place of the Great Death and can return to true life. Then we realize true rebirth for the first time, and with that we can realize true life. In Zen we do not compliment and flatter and build someone up. In Zen we teach the student to do what has to be done.

So many people still read books and learn explanations that say to look at this koan this way or that way. That is all reasoning and dualistic knowledge and information. That is not Zen. We have to reach the limit of words and do zazen to find true understanding. No matter what we say, we do not reach the true essence until there is nothing left to say; only when we have reached that place can we do zazen with our life on the line in one straight line. Then we work on one koan with everything we are, completely and totally. Without even noticing it, we lose track of our bodies, and we lose track of any sense of the zendo as well; everything around us fades away. From morning until night, there is truly only the koan that we have been given. And then, as we dig in deeper, even the koan disappears. All that is left is the breath, and finally that disappears as well. This is the place of slashing through the great root—when there is no self left at all. We enter that state of mind where we are totally transparent. With no heaviness and nothing left to hold on to, we become like a clear mirror, like a crystal palace.

This state of mind comes forth of itself. It has to be entered once, and from there we die completely. But this is not the final point. That full, ripened, and taut state is touched by something, and we burst forth—unable to stop laughing and knowing that the sentient beings are numberless and vowing that great Bodhisattva vow to save all of them.

THE PATH TO BODHIDHARMA

When Kyogen heard the sound of the tile on the bamboo it was not taught to him by his teacher or by his parents or by a book—it was his own mind. He knew that essence for himself. How can it be expressed to others? We do not know. The state of mind that cannot be explained comes from a place of no thoughts or ideas—just that clunk; the source of that which is unnameable—so we call it Buddha Nature.

When we are separated from all of our thoughts, this is Original Mind, and because we cannot explain it, we call it "Mu." From that state of mind of Mu, that sound of clunk jumped forth. There is no beautiful or ugly there. Nor is there a fixed world of nothing at all; there is nothing to appear or disappear. Because it is unnameable we call it the Buddha Nature, and from there we laugh and cry, sleep and wake, without any attachment at all—it is a free way of living we call living in our Buddha Nature, "Never abiding in any place yet manifesting continually."

This True Nature is what Hakuin expresses in the opening line of the *Song of Zazen* as "All sentient beings are essentially Buddhas." This is not something that we attain from doing zazen and repeating the Buddha's name—we already have it from birth. Rinzai says, "If you want to be no different from the patriarchs and buddhas, then never look for something outside yourself." Rinzai also says that the mind is like a mirror, and that is why anything can be reflected in it. A mirror does not discriminate in its reflecting. If what is before it is a great mountain like Fuji, the mirror does not consider whether the image will fit. A man or a woman, old or young, Mount Fuji or a sesame seed, the water of the Pacific Ocean or a cup of water, a diamond or a piece of glass—all are equal. In a mirror, the large, the small, the beautiful, and the ugly are all reflected equally. Nothing is splendid or poor or luxurious or impoverished; it is all equal. This is the wisdom of equal reflection. In the mirror, a rich person, a poor person, an educated person, and an uneducated person are exactly the same. To see all equally, as a mirror, with that clear state of mind, is called the mysterious perception of all things as equal. As Hakuin says, "How bright and clear the perfect moonlight of the Fourfold Wisdom!"

A mirror, when a flower comes before it, reflects back a flower. If a bird comes before it, it reflects a bird. The mirror reflects each thing exactly as it is, without any discrimination, and when that thing is gone, it leaves no trace behind. The True Self is like this mirror. Everyone at birth is endowed with this mind of the Buddha. It is not something we learn at school; it is part of our basic fabric, and from the origin it is undefiled. As Hakuin puts it, "All sentient beings are essentially Buddhas."

As Hakuin also says, "Even those who have sat zazen only once will see all karma erased." Even if for only a few times you have worked creatively and inventively on doing this zazen of letting go of knowledge and awakening to that with which we are already endowed at birth, you will be able to see the results directly. "Realizing the form of no-form as form," you will be able to see that there was nothing to be caught by in the first place. The essential words being given here—"All sentient beings are essentially Buddhas"—are accompanied with this most important phrase, "Realizing the form of no-form as form." How to see that in its ultimate way is told to us in these words of Hakuin. Our breathing is very important, but what is this deep breath important for? It is important for us to be able to see that from the origin there has been nothing to be caught by, nothing to be stuck on, not even once.

Hakuin says, "Realizing the thought of no-thought as thought." At this time we can let go of all of that conceptualization and humbly use our greatest potential and our wisdom freely. This is our Original Mind, our True Nature. When we see a person who is sad and suffering, we are able to spontaneously comfort them. That Original Mind with which we have all been born is that mind where we can see somebody who is suffering and become one with the suffering, able to comfort that person by becoming one with him or her. In that very moment when we can be with someone as if there is no separation between us, we know well this place of realizing the form of no-form as form. In a vibrant and living way we can live in this state of mind.

"Realizing the thought of no-thought as thought, whether singing or dancing, we are the voice of the Dharma." If we are always caught by our various ideas about things, and about what is happening to us and what is going on around us, then we cannot become clear in this way. We are not suddenly born in this very moment. Many millions of years of life from the very beginning of the universe have led up to this moment, and within each of us there are all the many components of our subconscious and our gathered awareness. Within that awareness we hold the stains of all human beings. We have to cut that awareness away, to get rid of it from the root, or we will be passing it down to all the people who come after us. Because we are here, because we are alive, we have this awareness of an "I," but at the same time, if we do not cut that away completely, we will not be able to experience this place free from all egoistic filters.

From the times of old we have Engo Kokushi's calligraphy with the words of Daito Kokushi and Hakuin Zenji's calligraphy, which have been carefully preserved. There is also Miyamoto Musashi's Eight-view Daruma, with its letters that are so powerful not because they have been written skillfully but because a vast state of mind is coming forth from them. This state of mind affects us when we look at them. We are astonished that the mind of a man could become so vast, taut, and energetic that we can feel it even today in this calligraphy. We can only be amazed and deeply impressed. That which has no form is being manifested there. This state of mind is Zen and also is called the Buddha and is called life. Every human has this from birth, and we all have the same capability to encounter this Original Mind. Yet the majority of people cover this over with the ego.

From the olden days, people of the path have sought and followed the path of Zen, this path of suffering, to find an awakened teacher from whom to learn. "What is the ultimate teaching of Buddhism?" It is to see that Zen beyond form, that state of mind beyond form. "What is life?" Those teachers would give a great shout, or hold up a single finger, or hit many blows with a stick, or with their eyes look piercingly, glaring, and in that way only could it be expressed.

That which has no form is borrowing those techniques of form to express what cannot be put into words. This is where Zen and various other paths connect and where calligraphy and Zen join. Daito Kokushi's words, Hakuin Zenji's calligraphy, these states of mind and this energy, are still living and vivid. In fact, this state of mind of Zen is what Zen brings forth and develops. This is that highest quality of mind of all people and it is an important grace. Hakuin Zenji is teaching us about this important zazen when he says, "All sentient beings are essentially Buddhas."

Sesshin

AMONG HAKUIN'S talks that were preserved by his disciple Torei Enji are the teachings called the *Rohatsu Jisshu*. This is a collection of the teachings given on each night of the rohatsu osesshin, which is held in honor of the deep enlightenment of Shakyamuni and represents the culmination of the year's practice. Hakuin Zenji taught from his own experience to encourage his disciples and to give them energy for their practice. Through the first four nights, Hakuin's teaching is almost all about the breathing practice of susokkan. He was teaching his students the very basics of the zazen practice and expressing to them clearly and emphatically the importance of susokkan, as we have done here as well.

On the fifth night of the rohatsu osesshin, Master Hakuin begins,

Intensive training sessions known as sesshin *continue for periods of eighty, ninety, and one hundred twenty days. Since the goal of all those who take part is to clarify the great matter, while the sesshin is in progress no one leaves the temple gates, and no one speaks unnecessarily. Practice is carried on with a spirit of dauntless, indomitable courage.*

Sesshin means to directly encounter one's mind, to touch one's mind; the word also expresses the gathering together of mind. This is not something we can do in our day-to-day lives. During sesshin, we must separate ourselves from all daily routine; we must touch directly, encounter directly, that very place from which the mind comes forth. Therefore, when we do sesshin, we must leave behind all connections to our daily and social life, or it is not a sesshin.

Although the traditional Japanese sesshin, or *ango*, was for as long as 120 days, at Sogenji a sesshin is for a period of one week. During a sesshin, each of the seven days has its own meaning: The first day is for starting off; the second is for putting forth our full energy. By the third day we are getting used to it all, but throughout the first four days we have a hard time with our bodies. By the fifth day we are a little tired, but we have become accustomed to our legs hurting. Remember, though, at this point it is not about having only two more days to go, but that this day comes only once. We must understand this. On the sixth day, seeing the end, we finally put forth everything we have. The seventh day is the last stretch. We cannot do our practice vaguely or haphazardly—to do so would be a waste of sesshin days. Our life is being shaved off by the second! We must understand how to use the sesshin in the best possible way.

Putting aside everything, facing straightforward, we work inventively and creatively to encounter the true source of mind. During the time of sesshin, everything in one's life is put aside in order to clarify this Great Matter, the most important issue, the problem of life and death. This is not about how to make today's living or how to solve emotional problems. If, while we are young, we can just once cut through to the deep root of life, then life becomes centered and clear; no matter what ideas or life plans we have held to this time, they all dissolve at this moment. We must realize that ultimate place, that very essence of our existence; we have to directly encounter that which actually lives through us. For this, all of our life within society must be cut off, separated from totally; only facing in the inner direction of our True Mind, we continually cut subtly and refine.

We do not go anywhere during this time. Because social rules must be observed when we go outside, in order to realize our true nature directly, we do not leave the place where we are doing sesshin. Even if during this time there is takuhatsu, or going into the community for alms gathering, people of practice wear deep hats that come down low, blocking their line of vision. By putting our line of sight at the feet of the person in front of us, we work energetically, even while walking, on directly encountering the true energy that lives through all of us. During the time that I was training at Shofukuji monastery in Kobe, President Kennedy was assassinated. A month later, without having heard any news of this, I saw a piece of newspaper lying in a gutter on which the terrible news was written; only then did I know of the tragic incident. Dojos are for the purpose of doing this—to completely cut oneself off from the outside world, and for the first time to even in the slightest way directly encounter that clear True Mind.

"[And] no one speaks unnecessarily." Given this clear-cut purpose, people during sesshin do not chatter and gossip idly; they are there for the sole purpose of clarifying that most important matter, putting their lives on the line for this. Talk of rules, directions, or corrections is allowed, but if we indulge in unnecessary conversation, then it is the same as completely letting go of our mind's true source.

Hakuin Zenji then continues: "Practice is carried on with a spirit of dauntless, indomitable courage." This is how he puts it. This is the fulcrum of practice; the central most important quality of practice is that we do it bravely, without wavering. We cannot do it with a weak heart, full of hesitation; nor can we do it while being concerned with what is to the left or to the right, or with what others are doing or thinking, with our physical problems or with how we feel about things, or how insecure we might feel—if we pay attention to each and every thing that comes along, there is no way we can possibly encounter that true source of mind, cut that root of life and death, or clarify the essence of what it really is to exist. Our training is not a scholarly study. We are not sitting to absorb philosophical information. If we wanted to do that we could go to college. We are not doing this for information, but to separate from that dualistically oriented mind. We have to completely throw all of that away, or we cannot encounter directly that true root of our life energy.

Everybody is always being deluded by the superficial shadow of this matter, believing that the shadow is the genuine thing. When it is our very mind that is giving birth to the whole world, we falsely think that it is the world that moves us. This is the great confusing source of so much delusion. But if we want to actually see that place from which all life energy comes, we have to cut off all external connection, cut away all worlds that concern us—at least once, cut them all cleanly away. Then, not holding a single concern within—not having a single trace of anything remaining whatsoever in our minds—we are able to become totally pure and clear. We have to cut subtly and refinedly to this place, to become pure and clear to this degree, or it all ends up being a big waste of time.

In recent years there was a man in a village near here who carved a stone image of Fudo the Immovable. He enshrined it beside a waterfall in the mountains of Yoshiwara.

Next, Hakuin gives an excellent example of someone who determinedly realized the pure and clear state of mind. At the time of Hakuin, when he lived in the town of Hara at Shoinji, there was a town a slight distance away called Okitsu; farther beyond that was an area called Iihara, where, in a small village, there lived a well-known man named Heshiro. He was rich and educated and was one of the responsible men of the town. In fact, he held responsibility for the whole town. In the mountain behind the town was a waterfall; at the spot where the falling water met the water in the pool below, the people of the town wanted to place a statue of Fudomyo—the guardian god

SESSHIN

who is firm and unmoved, expressing anger at dualism and extraneous thinking. When Heshiro heard that, he offered the money to have the statue carved. There was to be a celebration at the unveiling of the statue, which was then to be placed at the foot of the waterfall. Everyone in the town was invited; they were eating and drinking sake in honor of the day, and all of the guests were having a good time, when suddenly Heshiro was struck by something. As he looked up and down at the waterfall—as the water fell into the pool below and as foam rose—he saw many bubbles coming and going. He did not have any particular intention of looking at these bubbles, but suddenly he became aware of something.

One day, as he was watching the water tumbling down the cliffside, his gaze fixed on the bubbles that formed in the pool at the foot the falls. Some moved over the water for a foot or so before disappearing, some for two or three feet, and some continued floating two or three yards. Watching their progress, the man's past karma enabled him to perceive the impermanence of worldly existence.

When he looked at those bubbles he noticed that, while some flowed along for two or three meters before bursting, others would go on for ten or twenty meters. These bubbles were all born and flowed on and then disappeared. As he watched this happening, Heshiro thought, "This is very interesting! While they are all born together, some pop and disappear right away and some flow on for many meters." The very same bubbles born at the same time. This suddenly made him think of something else: *"The realization shook him to the marrow of his being. He now found it impossible to find peace within himself."* He realized that the exact same thing was true for all humans: We are all born with the same great birth cry, but there are some who die in birth, some who die at age three or five, some who die just after reaching adulthood—in the prime of their lives—and some who reach a ripe old age of eighty or ninety years. The lives of humans are the same as these bubbles. We are all born the same, but we never know when we are going to die. Seeing it like this, he was suddenly struck by the fact that everybody eventually dies; in spite of all of our differences, we will all burst and disappear! *"The impact of this realization made him feel the worthlessness of just living, just spending his days without understanding the mystery of life."* He then was struck again: Wait! That means I am going to die, too! It is true for me, too! I am going to die! For the first time he had seen his own death in front of him, and he could not sit still, knowing that he would also die. But he had no idea when. Everyone knows this in their heads, but how few actually understand this from the very marrow of their bones—no one applies this fact to the deep knowing of their own eventual death. No, this is not something that we can easily understand and accept even when we try to do so.

In the *Diamond Sutra* it says: "Thus shall ye think of all this fleeting world: a star at dawn, a bubble in a stream; a flash of lightning in a summer cloud, a flickering lamp, a phantom and a dream." All is empty, and if we do not see this as something that relates to ourselves, we will be continually deluded by shadows and by reflections, by this fleeting world. "Thus shall ye think of all this fleeting world." If we do not look closely at this we will never see the true, actual essence of it. The Buddha said this himself. People who enter training come in many different forms and varieties. They have their own personalities, which they want to improve; they have a life they want to live correctly; they come with many problems. But they must all understand the fleeting transience of all things, this impermanence of all things always passing along—that in all things there is nothing that can be depended upon. We must see this, know it as the ultimate first point before we enter training, or in the middle of the training we will quit, without exception. This has been said from ancient times.

SESSHIN

Heshiro of Iihara felt this deeply and directly—it became his very own problem, clearly relating to himself. He became suddenly very insecure and anxious. Shotoku Taishi in the seventh century also said, "All things in this world are nothing but a dream, a fantasy." It is all shadows, nothing is true, unless we can directly touch this very True Mind at its source, in every instant, that true Source of life energy. If we do not realize this, then everything is false; everything is a shadow given forth around that truth—merely that. Heshiro of Iihara became very anxious. He could not possibly eat delicious food and drink sake when he did not know how long he would be alive. No matter what he thought or did it all felt meaningless. This is the ripening of true karmic conditions—when we know and feel deeply that we have to train right now and cannot do anything else.

Some years ago there was a woman who died of cancer named Atsuko Chiba. In her autobiography she wrote that if any person goes through an experience of coming close to dying, afterward their way of life becomes simpler. They understand that we cannot know if we will be alive tomorrow or not. Social success, material comfort, or the sense that there is something that has to be done—all this becomes meaningless. One thinks about what one has been born to do, or what one wants to do in the time one has left. In this way she wrote, and it is truly just like this. Heshiro became deeply insecure. What meaning was there to any of it? He made excuses to leave the celebration early and go home. As he walked alone down the mountain, he thought about what he had to do to express this realization in the rest of his life. How was he going to live it? This is what he contemplated as he walked down that mountain, and just as he was thinking about this he passed in front of a house from which he could hear the sound of a sutra being chanted inside.

He chanced to hear a man recite a passage from the

THE PATH TO BODHIDHARMA

Dharma Words of Priest Takusui: "Courageous beings attain Buddhahood in a single instant of thought; lax and indolent beings take three long kalpas to attain Nirvana."

This was very mysterious. Here he had just been wondering how to live his life in the best possible way, and these words came into his ears—these words from the sayings of Master Takusui. "Courageous beings attain Buddhahood in a single instant of thought"—everyone who really puts their lives on the line with true bravery, everyone who does this wholeheartedly and with everything they have, will without fail find the resolution to their problem. "Lax and indolent beings take three long kalpas to attain Nirvana." However, someone who does this while keeping another world going at the same time—living a social life, just putting a little time aside for practice—will never taste the true flavor of that subtle ultimate place of being on the razor's edge. If we are going to do it, it has to be done all in one fell swoop. To carry it along limply for many attempts or hundreds of years has no meaning and will only be a total waste of time, never bringing us to a deep, clear resolution or enabling us to find true understanding. If you are going to do it, do it totally and completely—this is what the sutra was saying. Heshiro saw that this was how it had to be done and made up his mind to do it.

A great, burning determination rose in him. He entered the bathing room and shut the door behind him. Sitting down, he straightened his spine, clenched his fists, opened his eyes wide, and began doing zazen with great determination.

To be able to respond in this way, for his firm determination to be brought forth so totally, was not a result of that one brief realization at the waterfall. He must have had some preparation, some ground already settled. Although he worked in society, at the same time he had deep in his mind a question that he had to clarify. In his everyday life there must have been some basis for this to be able to happen. Because of this he was able to grab hold of this chance and with it establish this firm and solid immovable determination. This determination was transformed into the energy of an instant with which he was able to make the decision to totally change his life. The problem and the important point is this: Humans all have a life plan, believing that they should live this way and do these things that way; but to put everything they have, everything there is, into this one *nen*, this one moment, is what makes the difference between whether one can do this or not. He did this. "He entered the bathing room and shut the door behind him." He went into the guest bathroom, which ordinarily no one would use. He locked the door tightly; he made his spine tall and straight—although he never had any instruction on how to do zazen he imitated what he had seen. He straightened his back and gripped his fists and opened both eyes wide, looking straight ahead, at a spot on the floor a meter or a meter and a half in front of him. He opened his eyes so wide that light could fill them—it has to be like that or we will lose to pain and distraction. He did pure zazen, not letting anything distract him or concern him, nothing added on, not doing it to stabilize his life or to become happier or to improve the quality of his mind, not for any of that, just putting everything he had into it, no matter what came along—there was only this zazen, nothing else existed. He was determined to do it this way and to keep going.

Delusory thoughts flew thick and fast through his mind. The obstructions of the demon realms rose up to confuse him. But because he threw himself body and soul into the great Dharma battle, he finally severed life at the roots and entered into the formless realm of deep samadhi.

Of course, just sitting is not as easy as it sounds. All kinds of thoughts come up, all kinds of sayings, all kinds of delusions and ideas. All kinds of problems are always coming to interrupt zazen, one after another the thoughts come out: we question whether what we are doing is doing any good, or how long do we have to do it, or if we are doing it right, or whether it is really going to work or not. Or we think about all the other things we still have to do, about whether it is really necessary for our legs to hurt this much, about how nothing will come of tomorrow if we only do this. All these things and more. Then, if our mind becomes quiet, we start enjoying the fact that we are feeling good. Our body may feel like it's floating in air or being pulled into the ground; all kinds of strange sensations may intrude. As they come up, one after another, we have to just cut and throw away, cut and throw away, on and on and on and on . . . and doing this we go deeper and deeper.

For this we also have the excellent tools of susokkan and the koan. Just trying to be peaceful and quiet by itself will not bring about samadhi. "Delusory thoughts flew thick and fast through his mind. The obstructions of the demon realms rose up to confuse him. But because he threw himself body and soul into the great Dharma battle, he finally severed life at the roots and entered into the formless realm of deep samadhi." MU . . . MU . . . mu . . . mu . . . mu . . . mu . . . sometimes using power, sometimes intensively using our ki, pouring everything we have totally into it. And at that point . . . Will we retreat? Will we continue refining? This is the ultimate point. We cannot retreat here; we have to take it just one step further. To take it on through to its final place requires the "straightforward bravery" about which Hakuin always teaches us. He is teaching this from his own experience—to break through this place only straightforward bravery will work. Anybody can do the kind of zazen that looks peaceful and comfortable. There are lots of people all over the world who love to do zazen. But ninety-nine percent of them are not doing real zazen. They are sitting to become happier and to feel good. There is no real zazen there. Doing zazen begins

SESSHIN

when you become unable to know where to go and what to expect. Then, for the first time, you can take that straightforward bravery and pierce through. This experience is the only way to get that ticket to pass through the gate.

"He finally severed life at the roots and entered into the formless realm of deep samadhi." This is the most important point. Most people think that if they sit quietly their bodies and thoughts will disappear, but it does not work like that. It is not that easy. If it were that easy you could sleep or take drugs and do it. If you could just vaguely and lackadaisically sit on the cushion, doing nothing, and lose track of everything, then anybody would be able to do it. To really cut through the very root of life and death, to really get rid of that small self, one must experience and go beyond the limits of that small self. If we do not cross that boundary, we cannot taste the true flavor of this experience. To actually experience losing track of the zendo and of the people around us, to lose any sense of our bodies—if we cannot experience that we cannot pass through the barrier. But Heshiro did just that.

At first light, hearing the sparrows chirping around outside the building, he found that body had completely disappeared. Suddenly he saw his eyeballs pop from their sockets and fall to the ground. He felt the pain of his fingernails gouging into the palms of his hands, and realized his eyes were back in their proper place. He rose from his cushion and began to walk about. He continued to practice in the same manner for three nights. On the third night, when daybreak came and he got up to wash his face, he noticed that the trees in the garden were now somehow totally different. He consulted the priest of a nearby temple about it, but the priest was unable to provide any answers.

He had lost track of his body, but he had no idea how he had done it or what had happened. Somehow it had become morning. The birds were singing in the garden. "Chirp, chirp—

chirp, chirp," he heard the sparrows, but for some reason it felt as if they were chirping inside his own abdomen. His whole body had become the sparrow. It was so incomprehensible! So mysterious! He felt the birds' voices with his whole body, but there was no body—only the chirp of the birds! There was nothing he could do about it. It was as if his eyes were stuck to the ground; he had opened them wide when he sat, and that was all that was left of his body. How strange! Only a consciousness was remaining. After a while he returned to his usual way of seeing things. He could feel his body again. When his tightly gripped fists were loosened, he could feel the pain where his fingernails had been digging in, and he could feel the pain in his legs. He came back to normal and moved his body; he could finally stand up. "How strange that was! I've never felt anything like this before! It is really hard to understand! But it feels so good! So clear and fresh. This is interesting; I'll do it again!"

On the spot he started again. And while cutting and throwing away, cutting and throwing away over and over again, he again lost track of everything. His body again disappeared, the scenery all around him again disappeared. Again he did not know what had happened, but he lost track of it all completely, and again there was the morning dawning. This went on for three days and three whole nights! On the morning of the third day, as he went to wash his face after getting up from sitting, he looked at the garden and said, "This is very funny! Very strange! What's happening here! The whole garden is shining! I've never seen the garden like this and I've been looking at it every single day! I've never seen it look this beautiful before! How weird! The trees are shining! The leaves are shining! Everything in the whole garden is shining—even the rocks are shining! This is really interesting—I've never seen it look like this before!"

Heshiro went to tell the local Zen priest about his unusual experience. He described it to the priest and asked him

SESSHIN

what he thought or knew about it. He asked the priest what it meant. But the priest said he had never had such an experience himself; he had never passed through that barrier; he did not understand, so he could not tell Heshiro anything about it. "The kind of sitting you have just done and that kind of experience . . . I've never done it! That's a pretty amazing experience you've had! Hakuin Zenji lives in Hara at Shoinji Temple and he had deep experiences like this. He has really experienced that enlightenment of the Buddha. You should ask him about it—he'll know what to tell you—that's the best idea." This is what the priest told Heshiro, so Heshiro decided to go and see Hakuin while his experience was still fresh and alive in him.

He then decided to come and see me [Hakuin]. He set out for Shoinji in a palanquin. Upon reaching the high pass at Satta, the splendid prospect of the ocean at Koura came into view far below. At that instant he knew beyond any doubt that what he had grasped was the truth that plants and trees and the great earth all attain Buddhahood. Proceeding to my temple, he passed through the fires of my forge, and subsequently penetrated a number of koan barriers.

Heshiro called a carriage and hurriedly left to go to Shoinji. The mountain road was steep, and they stopped frequently to rest. After leaving Okitsu and passing through Yuigahama, at the top of a steep hill was a place where one could look out and see Mount Fuji clearly on a ridge, with the lake called Tagaura in full view just below. At that place, with that beautiful scenery so clearly visible, he noticed, "I've passed through here many times before, but it has never looked like this!" It was so beautiful and wonderful it was as if he was seeing it for the first time. "It is so beautiful! I've heard about this somewhere before—when the Buddha attained enlightenment he said: 'How wondrous! How wondrous! All beings, without exception, are endowed from the origin with the same bright, clear mind to which I have just been awakened! How incredible! The trees, the birds, the grasses! They are all shining—everything is full of this life energy—the True Nature is illuminating and shining through everything!'" He had heard that the Buddha had spoken thus when he realized his deep enlightenment. "I know I've heard that and this is just like that! Let's hurry up here! I want someone to hear about this and tell me what this experience is about!"

He again hurriedly proceeded to Hakuin's temple. When he arrived there, he was invited in and described his experience to Hakuin. Hakuin said: "It is a deep experience, but not yet complete." At that point Hakuin questioned him on two or three of the patriarchs' koans. He answered them precisely and on the spot, as if they were his very own questions and he had already lived the answers himself. Hakuin confirmed, "This is the real thing, not just a one-shot momentary glimpse! This is not just some abnormal state of mind—this is the real thing." This is what Hakuin said in affirmation.

He was an ordinary man, with no prior knowledge of Zen practice whatever. Yet in just two or three short nights he achieved a realization. The great victory he gained in the struggle against delusory thought was the result of courageous determination and single-minded resolve.

This Heshiro was just a normal person; he had never studied Buddhism, but just worked every day of his life at a job. Yet in three days of totally determined sitting he had broken through and resolved the Great Matter. Bravely and straightforwardly cutting through and throwing away every single extraneous thought and delusion that arose—without stopping—he was not led astray by anything that came along. This is Zen. It is not a scholarly study or some kind of special knowledge. It is only facing directly that source from which our life energy arises, clarifying completely that root of our very being alive.

SESSHIN

Only this one moment. To do this requires straightforward bravery—and only that. There is only one way in which it can be done: You must cut it all and throw it all away, continually doing that and only that. That is what it is about. If not that, what will you do when you die? Complaining will not work then. You have to make that determined effort now. You have to die whether you want to or not.

The great victory he gained in the struggle against delusory thought was the result of courageous determination and single-minded resolve. How can you, full-fledged Zen monks, fail to generate this same fierce and dauntless spirit?

Hakuin says to all of us: "Why don't you do it? What are you waiting for? That waiting will never get you anywhere—even if you spend your whole life at it, you'll only be chasing shadows!"

Enlightenment

THE ESSENTIAL POINT of any religion must be whether or not one has a true, deep, and actual experience of the Original Nature. As Kanzan Egen said in his final words, "I ask that you work only on the Great Matter." This is beyond any need for explanation. We can still partake today of the "rice," the essence of the Buddhadharma, because every single patriarch, with clear purpose and fiery determination, thoroughly chewed and digested this rice of the Buddhadharma so as to feed and raise others in the truth. It is that deep compassion that has kept this rice feeding us to today.

Religious people of today have a legitimate concern about the lack of true essence in their religions. We have become more and more easily confused in our search for this essence and do too many things, always looking externally. We must look inside and not become self-important and proud. Kanzan, knowing that what he said was already an overstatement, an unnecessary explanation of an unstatable truth, said, "I ask that you work only on the Great Matter." The Buddha and Bodhidharma taught the same thing. From this same enlightenment experience came all the teachings of the Dharma.

Today's young people look for satisfaction in sex and, when they are a little older, in fame and money, but when these things have been obtained, what is left? We have simply become older and we find ourselves in a meaningless state. If there is no living function for religion in our lives, then religion becomes useless. Sex, fame, and money may bring us pleasure, but it is only pleasure of the moment. Such pleasure is transient and always fades away. True religion is also of this moment, but it has a changeless form extending from the past through the future, an absolute center unchanged by external occurrences. For people to have times of temporal enjoyment is fine, but if that changeless root, that experience of the clear mind, is not also realized, then, as we age, we begin to feel more and more that our life is already over. This happens because we live in a world of pleasure instead of a world of each day's joy beyond temporal pleasure.

No matter what path you follow to reach the place of truth, the place you arrive at is the same. When people are totally committed to their religious practice, they no longer need to be chauvinistic about it. All that is necessary is to dig into that basic question, to reach that deepest essence, and humbly accept Grace. This path is not about searching for information but about reaching for those answers and knowledge that are not limited by such names as Hinduism, Buddhism, Judaism, and Christianity. When one still needs to hang on to a sect, then one has only a shadow of the real thing, a mere reflection of a religion that does not constitute a true and deep understanding of it. The true understanding takes place prior to the teaching of any religion. We must reach that place of true humanity, that place where we can truly realize that the life energy of every single person has exactly this very same root. This state of mind is beyond explanation and teaching with words and phrases. It cannot be spoken about; it can only be realized through each person's individual experience.

For those who have realized this place, there is nothing more to search for externally, or to find in another religion. All people in society need to realize this true human nature—not Buddha, or God, or that self that yearns for sex, fame, and

ENLIGHTENMENT

money, but that which would naturally be respec[ted by any] who came in contact with it. Directly feeling the g[reat] clarity of this true human nature, we bow not on[ly] to Buddha but to that holy human quality that does not come from a life spent napping and yawning. To say "that person can do it but I cannot" is indulgent and comes from not looking at things in the right way and living in accord with that way.

When you can clarify and realize your own deepest essence, that is what will give you a clear understanding of the essence of others. Here is the central, most important point and the truth of what is being done in the practice of Zen. If we train only for ourselves, for our own improvement, for our own enlightenment, for our own awakening, then our training energy will not continue with the same momentum. And why is this? It is because in thinking only of ourselves we are cutting up and dividing the total life energy.

When we have made a vow that burns intensely within us, when we feel more deeply than anything else that we must train and work for all beings, then no matter what occurs it will not obstruct us. But when our vow wavers and weakens, even a small matter will become a great obstruction. For this reason, above everything else, first and foremost, people of the Way must raise a great determined vow. We vow that no matter what happens we will work until we realize the truth of our Original Nature and illuminate all with it, and to do that we must enter samadhi. If we do not hold this vow firmly, it will not do. It will not work if we vow with only a lukewarm commitment; our vow must be absolutely clear. If that vow comes as an egoistic expression, it will not work either, because the ego is out only for what is good for itself. For one brief period of time such a vow may bring energy, but that energy will always fade away. Because an egoistic idea is one that ultimately concerns only the ego, it puts society aside and has no regard for life's true source. This total life energy has to be clarified; if you are doing it only for your own small self-expression of it, it is useless. Only because your life energy and that of all people come from exactly the same source does this have any meaning.

The ultimate reality of Buddhadharma can never be actualized without the deepest vow—one that needs patience, perseverance, and endurance. And what is that mind, that vow? To not have a conceited mind is different from having a firmly committed mind, from having the determination to continue until the truth is understood. You cannot run away from reality. What is everyone really suffering from? There are many economic and political problems in the world today, but more basic is the suffering of the mind that has nothing to believe in, the continually anxious mind. Today, people do not believe in God and do not know where to turn. How easily men and women come together and then separate when they do not like each other anymore. It may be OK for them, but what about their children, many of whom do not even know who their parents are? What can they grow up believing? Knowing nobody thought about their birth and their life, how can they believe in anything? If everybody looks out only for his or her own pleasure and ignores the great problems such self-centeredness causes in society, where will that take us in the future? This is not somebody else's problem.

Today, elementary school children are victims of drug dealers. Young children are being kidnapped and raped. What has happened to the basic standards of human beings? If we do not realize the True Mind within ourselves, then who will? If we can think in terms of realizing this True Mind, then how can we worry about something so small as our own hunger or our own aches and pains? If we can think like this then we will certainly realize the fulfillment of our path. Our training must be done in this way or there is no meaning in it whatsoever. When we know

ENLIGHTENMENT

what we must do for all of humanity, without falling back one step, then we can continue and fulfill our purpose. This must be our firmest vow. If one of us realizes the True Mind, it is for all beings in the Ten Directions. You must realize it to this point without fail!

If we cannot attain kensho, if we do not experience enlightenment, it is because we have not yet made that firm commitment. It is because we have not yet with total, deep determination taken that sharp stance that will enable us to cut through everything that comes along. By always moving according to our surroundings—the day-to-day conditions, preconceived time limits, and the circumstances in which we find ourselves—we lose our resolve, we do not make the efforts necessary to take our practice to completion. And because we do not make our determination totally firm, we give up in the middle—that is why we do not experience kensho. If we have true bravery and take our practice to its final point, it will work—no matter who it is that is doing it. There is not a single person in the world for whom enlightenment is impossible; if we sincerely put our lives on the line, each and every one of us can realize it. Anyone can encounter True Mind.

Where this idea of enlightenment often becomes a problem is when everyone reads the writings of both the old and the present-day masters and they take this one experience and place it in a conceptual framework. They just pluck out the idea of this excellent or seemingly magical experience and think, "That's what I want." What is overlooked are the years of practice and, behind that one experience, the years of very plain learning and of cutting through everything and anything that comes along before that clarified state of mind is experienced. Today, people take drugs to induce the very same states of mind that a person can reach in the midst of deep meditation. But to use drugs to reach such states of mind is like riding a helicopter to the top of

THE PATH TO BODHIDHARMA

a mountain. When you reach the top of the mountain you can see the scenery. But you will not know the essence one experiences in the process of walking up the mountain one footstep at a time; you do not know how to reach the top of the mountain on your own. Looking at it from the point of view of the Buddha, taking drugs to change one's state of mind has no meaning. If the experiences one must know to reach that state of mind are not passed through, then what is the value of realizing that state of mind? The scenery may look the same from the top of that mountain, but those who have not climbed the mountain for themselves have lost the chance to understand those things about themselves that are in fact the main point of the process. People want to go straight to the mountain top, they want to go for this one special occasion of kensho without looking at the step-by-step process that comes before it. They decide that kensho is what they are going after, and that is what the entire process is about. This is why enlightenment is viewed as such an extraordinary part of the process, rather than being properly looked at as just the next step in a long, ongoing process.

Someone who is learning archery goes through a similar process. At the beginning one faces the target, puts an arrow in the bow, and shoots, but one hardly ever hits the target, let alone the bull's-eye. By doing it over and over, repeating the same process again and again, learning and perfecting the form, one improves very slightly and is able to begin to understand the best way to go about hitting the target. As one practices in this way, the arrow begins to hit the target more frequently. This ripening, this becoming accustomed to the way it is done, is something that occurs naturally over time. Without being self-consciously aware of what we are doing, we learn to be more skillful. Yet in this midst of learning we are unaware of the entire process.

Practice is the same. Doing the susokkan practice, you wonder what meaning there could be in counting numbers.

ENLIGHTENMENT

What is this thing called breathing? Even though it belongs to you, you do not understand it. And even when you begin to understand how to go about it, you cannot do it in a satisfactory way; you just cannot do the breathing in the way you want to. Yet eventually, little by little, you begin to understand how to do it. That breath that you did restlessly and in so much confusion becomes more and more settled and clear. You develop a taut and fulfilled state of mind. Your mind becomes deeper and sharper in quality. In this way you continue, vowing always that you will not stop until you have attained the very final realization.

And when the susokkan has thoroughly deepened—both the breath and the mind—you can settle into your koan directly and with everything you have. If it is not done in this way, the counting of the breaths is only empty repetition, or the koan is only a mechanical questioning. But if you can reach this point, then by using the koan as a sword for cutting off all thoughts, you can continue unceasingly from morning to night and from night until morning, doing it over and over until you do not know where you are or even what you were just doing, with no self-conscious awareness remaining, becoming totally involved in that One. You do not even feel your own body. When your mind is truly clear the pain in your legs goes away. Your breath, your counting even—they also disappear. Only the clearest mind, with not the smallest speck of awareness in it, remains.

This ultimate place of awareness is what is called samadhi. In the Buddha's experience this place has to be passed through. We let go of all the random thoughts that clutter our minds. We gather our intense focus and cut through all past conditioning, the dualism and unnecessary information, until there is no place for it to remain. Eventually we become completely serene and tranquil, with no more sense of a body or of a self.

THE PATH TO BODHIDHARMA

Joshu called this state of mind Mu because that is all there was to be said—not because there is some meaning in the word, but because this state of mind could not be expressed in any other words. But this state of mind continually deepens until finally even this Mu disappears. That is also a place we have to pass through. Until then we become vague, then sharp, then vague; our inner essence becomes strong, it fades, it comes back again, but we cannot throw our hands up in despair and quit and retreat at this point.

We have to realize this essence all the way to that tranquil place of no awareness of seeing or hearing, of quiet serenity. But first we have to know that Great Death, that place of no internal and external differentiation. Yet this is still not it. We have then to see that which has created the universe, or we have not experienced the true Buddhadharma. We have to die to the place from which the universe was born. And if we realize this, then we are reborn—our purified consciousness is reborn. As Mumon Ekai says, then suddenly that tranquil place erupts in a way to shatter the heavens and make the earth tremble. We are once more reborn; the mountains are reborn, the stars are reborn, the rivers are reborn, the people around us are reborn. Our whole mind is this universe and full of wonder, full of joy. When the Buddha saw the morning star he was full of this same wonder and joy. When Hakuin heard the sound of the morning bell ringing, he had the same feeling. And when Kyogen heard the tile hit the bamboo he also, in full awe and wonder, heard the joy of this sound. They all experienced this deep wonder. And where that is clear, there is nothing to be afraid of. There is no concept of God or Buddha, there are no patriarchs to be in awe of, no words to be played around with.

If you can continue with your deep vow, never lessening your intensity and not giving up, putting everything you have into it, then all of your desires, delusions, and attachments, one

ENLIGHTENMENT

after another, will fall away. From within your deepest mind you can experience for yourself the Original Nature. You can encounter the deepest source of Zen and Buddhism; from your own experience you can see that true essence in every aspect, arising from your own life energy and revealed before you. You can understand how your life energy, just as it is, is expanding throughout the universe. You can tell that there is not even the slightest difference between your life energy and that of others. You can know clearly for yourself, not just conceptually, that everyone shares the same life energy, that everyone's energy comes from the same root.

This experience is something that is available to everyone. This Original Nature can be realized if you can just let go of everything. To conceptualize about this is meaningless. While still in our world you must hold on to nothing—not a single thing—but let go of your attachments to every possession, every pain, every plan, every material thing, all of your self-centered opinions, separating yourself from all decoration. When you can truly become that state of mind, this is in itself an astonishing experience, full of great wonder. There is a great joy in this, and it will fill you with gratitude when you realize it for the first time.

This is something that cannot be explained in words. It is like the air around us. Who remembers to be thankful for the air we breathe? We all take it for granted. No one notices the air or thinks to say thank-you to it, but whether we notice it or not, it is always there. Those who do notice know the joy of always being supported by it; they know gratitude and joy with each breath. When one approaches the experience of enlightenment only intellectually, trying to grasp some idea of it with the mind, every day will remain filled with dissatisfaction and suffering, because one cannot experience this joy merely by thinking about it.

If one truly awakens, then those long years of effort and work result in awakening to the true deepest Original Nature. The moment we know this it is realized completely. In this very moment, in this one instant, at this time. All of the attachments that have obstructed our minds until that moment—the delusions, the opinions that things had to be like this or like that, the dualistic ideas of the past—all of it falls away in that one moment, disappearing completely. This awakening comes both suddenly and not suddenly. For those who can throw it all away, throw everything away, it happens every day. For those who cannot, no matter how many things, how many concepts, how many methods they accumulate, it will not occur. This process is about how we can live our everyday lives, and it is about what we hold important. It is about what we can let go of, how we can feel the joy of having nothing at all, of returning to the Original Nature. This is what will bring us to awakening. It has to be done by each and every person, and done totally. Especially in today's society—in which we are constantly overwhelmed with external stimulation—this stance of cutting totally to the roots of our problems and resolving them exactly where we are right now is very important. If we do not do this, it will be impossible to awaken, to understand directly the true value of being human, to have that true, deep, and actual experience of Original Nature.

Work and Society

IN TODAY'S SOCIETY, with its increasingly sophisticated uses of technology, everything is being organized by computers. We communicate with each other through computers and receive information through computers. Our lives are being programmed by computers, and we are feeling secure about it. When we are unwell, we go to the doctor; receiving medicine, we feel comforted. In human relationships as well, we are all seeking kindness and comfort; we are searching for some essence of security amid the turbulence and complexity of the world in which we live.

This is how insecure this era is, causing people to look for safety in everything they do. To put it a different way: Separated from reality, our thoughts are constantly running ahead of our actions in this present moment. Within all of this, Zen is to be quietly and steadily working, raising daikon radishes, growing leafy vegetables, raking the garden, pulling up weeds. Doing this, the truth is realized in all things. The living pulse of life that unites all things is realized in this. Zen is about sweating with your entire body and moving all of your limbs and every part of yourself, no matter what you are doing. Even when you find yourself in the most difficult and painful circumstances, to be unswerving and always raising this state of mind is Zen.

Rinzai Zenji taught us this especially when, at the end of the Tang dynasty, he himself was living in times of great economic confusion and rebellion in all of the various local

THE PATH TO BODHIDHARMA

religions. Everywhere temples were being demolished, statues of the Buddha were being destroyed, and sutra books were being burned. People of religion were forced to leave their posts; bribes and treachery in government were rampant. There was nothing whatsoever in the political establishments or in society in which one could find something to believe. God and Buddha, which should have brought refuge and something to believe in, were lost in the chaos, along with that to which everyone should be awakened: that True Person of No Rank within this lump of red flesh, that dung bag that will bleed if it is cut into, from morning until night that physical body we are always spending time with. That True Person of No Rank—beyond description or measure, the only one throughout the heavens and earth, just one human—isn't this where that true quality of being human is? That which has no rank and measure among humans—isn't this where that can be found? To awaken to this clear mind is what Rinzai taught.

Zen teaches labor first, but it is not just any old work or *samu*. Samu, everyone working together, is the basis of living Zen. And in that, what has to be realized is the most human quality that unites all people. If there is not an actual awakening to *this*, then the way of Zen becomes nothing but labor alone and that which has to be taught will lose its life. Within that labor there must be a polishing of *this* and a developing of the human being. This is where the essence of Zen must be found and be at work.

Dogen Zenji went to China at the age of twenty-four. At the age of twenty-eight, he put aside his training in China and returned to Japan. Upon his return, when asked what he had learned, he said, "Only this: In the morning the sun rises without thinking from the East; in the same way, our eyes are horizontal in our face. This I realized clearly. No one is exempt from this. Empty-handed I went and empty-handed I returned; there was not a single word of Dharma spoken. The sun rises in the morning in the east, the moon sets in the west, the rooster crows at the break of dawn, and every four years a leap year comes."

Dogen Zenji did not bring home any special statue of the Buddha to pray to and treasure; he did not bring home any special sutra book to read and treasure; he did not bring back any special item of great cultural value. He came home truly empty-handed. "I am alive right here." This clear realization of his life energy, just this understanding, was what he had been able to experience deeply. This same life energy rises as the sun in the east every morning; and in the evening it rises again in the east as the moon, and as the sun it sets in the west. Every four years another leap year comes around. This actual truth is all there is; anything besides this, anything with a fancy name like the Buddhadharma—"I know nothing about it." Dogen Zenji spoke like this, spoke about the natural, obvious way things are, about things just as they are.

Just as it is, our being alive right here, right now, at this very moment—we can receive this truth, the natural, obvious understanding of what that is. There is nothing besides that to be called a "Buddhadharma." If we do not know the actual life energy, alive and vivid in this very moment, we will never find something called a Buddhadharma. The Dharma is not about reasoning and intellect. The Buddha's Dharma is about life and how we live it. Separated from what is alive and living, there is no Dharma, it has no meaning. For a man there must be this man's purpose of life; for a woman, this woman's purpose. While we are all equal as human beings, we each have our own individual life to live, our own individual qualities of how to live. Parents have their own particular way of understanding things; children have their own responsibility to live as children. People have to act in the way that is most appropriate and natural for their situation. Schoolteachers have their own way of looking at life and how things should be done. For students, there is a student-like way of living, with the creative and inventive efforts that go along with learning in the best possible way. This obvious and natural way of things is the Buddhadharma. Obvious and natural things being done in a natural way—aside from that there is no Dharma.

During the Edo period, in the area of Kyushu called Hakata, there was a priest named Sengai. When some people asked this priest to write in calligraphy some words of felicitation for the New Year, he wrote:

> *Parents die*
> *Children die*
> *Grandchildren die*

The people for whom he had written this responded, "This isn't a very congratulatory message for the New Year! Talking about dying is not very felicitous." Priest Sengai replied with a cool look, "What do you mean it is not congratulatory? What is more felicitous—the parents die, the children die, then later the grandchildren die—what could be more natural and congratulatory than this? That it does not happen in the opposite order is the most felicitous thing!" This is how he explained it. The ways of nature are all expressed in just this natural, obvious way, and by seeing and accepting things in this way, mankind's base is laid.

However, in today's world, more and more this natural and simple way of seeing and being is disappearing. Dogen Zenji said that the rooster crows, signaling the breaking of dawn, but today we rarely have a chance to hear the crowing of a rooster. Unless a male bird is raised for some unusual reason, no one needs a rooster. We use eggs in our daily life, but the eggs are born from chickens who are raised on shelves, one hundred, two hundred, one thousand, ten thousand of them lined up, fed, and kept alive just to provide us with eggs. The world of chickens that was known by our parents or grandparents—when everybody had a chicken coop near the house, with the rooster and the hens running around the garden together cackling, and the children listening to this sound while they gathered eggs—this is something we seldom see anymore.

In those days, every egg that was laid without exception could become a chick. Today, the eggs that chickens lay do not become chicks; chickens have become nothing more than egg-laying machines. According to the needs of society, they merely lay the eggs. Those chickens who cannot lay eggs anymore are killed; they are machines, no longer something natural. For those of us who receive those eggs, it is as if our naturalness as humans has also disappeared. We no longer see cows, goats, and chickens raised among trees and grass. This natural and simple world has been replaced by the culture of technology and the convenience of living comfortably. One after another the things of nature are disappearing from view.

Perhaps the most famous of Zen's traditional texts is the *Ten Oxherding Pictures*. The ox, in India, is considered to be a holy living being; a servant of God, it is held in great reverence by both Hindus and Buddhists. Today we think of the ox or the cow as something to eat or the source of milk. But in the olden days the ox served as our very hands: the garden was tilled and planted and dug by this silent ox; without it the crops could not be planted. We did not forget that the ox was an animal, but it was also a friend and lived under our roof, and was taken good care of so it would not become sick. People fed the ox before they ate themselves and gave it a clean place to live. It was precious and could be depended upon. When the industrial revolution began, machines took over the jobs of the oxen, and the oxen that required so much care disappeared—and with them all those things we learned from them. Machines will not teach us to have a caring mind. The ox that did our work so patiently taught us to know that place in ourselves. To live like the ox, to not be superficial and shallow but to quietly do our work with depth and patience—how many of us have oxen around to learn this from?

Kanzan Egen said, "The Original Mind is great and round, why do we fall into delusion and darkness?" Everyone has the same mind as the Buddha and a clear Buddha Nature from birth. Yet if this is so, why do we become so deluded and confused? This is the challenge given in Kanzan's question. As a boy, Dogen Zenji went to Mount Hiei to study, but with this very question he was brought to a point of intense doubt. "The Original Mind is great and round, why do we fall into delusion and darkness?" From the origin we are all Buddhas, so why did we begin to be deluded? Such questions Dogen asked, but no one could answer him. Very near Mount Hiei lived a priest, Eisai Zenji, who had just come back from China. Dogen was told that while in China, Eisai Zenji had practiced Zen, and he would understand. So Dogen offered himself to the path of Zen.

Our original and true mind, our Original Nature and True Self just as it is, is, in Buddhism, called the great round mirrorlike mind. Our original mind has no shape and no form—the all-embracing mind is like a mirror embracing the entire universe, in which all sorts of shapes and forms are reflected. Rinzai Zenji teaches with clarity about how a mirror reflects what comes in front of it exactly and then retains no trace of anything after it is gone. The everyday practice of Rinzai Zenji is in this state of mind that leaves not a single bit of clutter behind. This is his clear mind and the Original Nature of each and every one of us: to enter fire without being burned, to enter water without drowning, to fall into hell and yet be as if we are playing gladly. Not being attached to anything we see, and not being deluded

WORK AND SOCIETY

by that which we hear—to live so that no matter what world we find ourselves in it is as if we are sightseeing—this state of mind is that of Rinzai. This is the Zen of Rinzai. At the same time, the *Rinzai-roku*, his collected writings, also teaches us a way of living our daily lives: to not add on a second or third *nen*, or associative thought, to the first nen. To do this is worth more than ten years of pilgrimage, he tells us. When those nen arise, simply do not add any associative thoughts to them. If you are angry, just leave it at that. If you are happy, just leave it at that. If you are sad, just leave it at that.

No matter how much we have we always want more. This greedy love that always wants more but will not let go of what it already has, all of this attachment, has to be cut, otherwise our lives are painful. Once we cut this need for attachment we can know peace of mind for the first time. We spend so much time with thoughts of our children and our bodies—this must be cut through, or we will never be liberated. All our thoughts must be thrown away—those lingering wisps of thoughts that are always flying back and forth—we must get rid of them and awaken to that true and clear mind with which we are all endowed. This is our guide to the liberation of our mind.

Getting rid of our thoughts is not about forcing ourselves not to think. We should not waste our efforts worrying "I shouldn't think this" and "I mustn't think that." It just means when you are angry, cut it away; when you are happy, cut it away; when you are sad, cut it away—again and again. If you can live so that you are not stopped by any of your thoughts or start adding further associations to them, it will be of more value than even ten years of pilgrimage. Every day of living will be free from attachments and obstructions. If we can live in the practice of this freedom it will have more value than ten years of zazen in the zendo. The deepest and most profound teaching of Zen is here: the way of life that holds on to nothing at all.

In the *Ten Oxherding Pictures* this clear mind—that which we have always had—is symbolized by the ox. The pictures begin at the point when the Bodhisattva mind has been awakened, and with the help of the Buddha's teaching we are able to let go of all our thoughts, even those we have so carefully gathered. We can then see that the mind's root is our own true source; as this becomes clearer and clearer, we are seeing the ox's footprints. We dig and dig to where there is nothing at all within our minds, reaching that place of caring for the ox. We think this is our clear mind, but we still become caught by the expressions of others and by what we hear and see. This mind must always be shepherded to keep it settled and centered. As we become able to tend it easily, it becomes the mind of riding the ox home. As we see and hear and live in our daily life in an innocent state of mind, we can be with the ox in its original state and be at home. Yet there is still a need for the ox. Eventually, however, we do not even need the ox; there is no need to even think about aligning our state of mind—this will occur naturally. There is no longer any self or ox to keep track of. The realization of this is that source of the mind of God and Buddha, but this is not yet absolute. From here we must go back into the world. If we stop here we will be ignoring the suffering of the world and just protecting our own happiness. This is why the tenth picture is necessary—where we feel it all with our clear mind.

This is that place of Kanzan's koan: "The Original Mind is great and round, why do we fall into darkness and delusion?" From that empty mind we see and hear and move and walk and feel with our whole bodies. We cannot separate ourselves from that reality; we are sentient beings, but whether we are deluded by and attached to this reality or not is what is important. Those who have let go of the small ego cannot be deluded any more by the world. They lose their attachment to it. While remaining in the same world there is an enormous difference—between heaven and earth they change from the world of attachment to the world of reality. But this is still not complete. We need to go and work hard with those people who are suffering and join them in their situations and experience their states of mind, yet we need to keep ourselves from being caught by any situation and attached to it. This is the state of mind of entering into the marketplace with open hands, of returning to where we started—though it is not really where we started at all.

It may seem as if we have become fools, but it is only that we are not attached to things. We are entering the world of close relationships between men and women but we are not attached to it—we remain wide open and free and unattached. That place has to be realized or it is not the real world of the Buddhadharma; if there is even a speck of a small self it becomes an attachment, and is not a way of liberating others. We have to always work creatively and inventively on how to let go of ourselves. All of our hate and resentment centering on our own small self have to be forgotten and thrown away, along with all those thoughts that we find difficult and uncomfortable. We have to let go and see the world exactly as it is. With new eyes we have to always see the truth of all things. And to do this these eyes have to be open. If everyone's eyes are open to this way of seeing, then how bright the world will become. We can easily blame others for our problems, bring up other people's faults, and worry about our mistakes, clinging to our thoughts about them. Zen is not about being irresponsible and ignoring things; it is about not becoming caught by the things we hold in our mind, about being able to remain unattached, about seeing clearly and beginning again and letting go of the mind that lingers on something over and over again. If we could all forgive and see each another with an open heart, see the mistakes we make ourselves, humbly and deeply looking at our own behavior, then how wonderful our lives together could be.

To see every single day, every meeting of every person and thing, and everything we do as fresh—this is the religious and spiritual way of life. This is not something that can be done instantaneously. The world of the mind cannot be realized in an instant. This is the mind we are endowed with for our entire life; to clarify and keep it bright is what we have this life for, and to sincerely and wholeheartedly do this is our responsibility for our entire life. This is what we need to do, the way the ox keeps his efforts going until the job is done.

If we are not careful we begin to think of our zazen and our life in society as two separate things. When we return to our usual place of living, our state of mind of zazen is left behind; it fades away. We see our friends and go into town, and our state of mind of zazen disappears. That is not the meaning of true zazen. No matter how much we talk to friends and no matter where we go or what we do, within that functioning our mind must always find the place to which it can return. That place of no stain whatsoever must always be worked on creatively and inventively. This essence must not be let go of, or it is not true zazen.

For most of us the tiredness of our mind is much greater than the tiredness of our physical body. The tiredness of our body will be relieved if we rest, but even when we rest the tiredness of our mind does not go away. When we suffer from the heaviness of a "self"—an attachment and opinion based on being stuck on the idea of a self—we crush many things in the world. It is as if we are running around all day adding clutter to our minds. And if by doing zazen we become heavier and darker, then we have a mistaken way of looking at it, we are chasing something far away. Zazen is not for making us dark and miserable but for realizing that there is nothing far away to be chased after. We must instead shave away what is unnecessary in every day's work. The more we do this the brighter and clearer and fresher we should become. To do zazen for a long time is to look brighter and easier. The point is not to do koans and think about things in a difficult way. Koans are made to be unsolvable intellectually. All koans are the same in this. We just shave everything away with the koan, leaving nothing at all behind. And with susokkan as well, we shave it all away with that. We think about how good our zazen is today, and how well our susokkan is going, but what if it is bad tomorrow? What happens then? We do koans to get rid of extraneous thoughts, but we can get rid of that clutter without doing koans as well. And if we do that we all come out at the same place. It is that same place that Bodhidharma pointed out when he said, "Nothing holy, only emptiness." We can do this by eating with no sense of our selves, by looking forward to what is for supper and finding it delicious, no matter what it is.

If in our minds we are truly bright and pure, completely empty and clear, then in this world there is nothing to be caught on. We can work and function freely and openly and be bright with that joy which is the brilliance of the radiant mind. From all parts of us great radiance will shine forth. Even though we give up the joy of wearing beautiful clothing, or savoring numerous flavors from a great feast, if we realize that clear and empty mind, even a patched cotton robe, just as it is, is a luxurious garment. Even oats and rice, with rice bran pickles—even what might seem such a small, plain meal—will become a great feast of a hundred flavors. In this way we can receive and experience everything that comes to us.

Takuan Zenji was a famous Japanese Zen master. He had a disciple who wrote a famous text on the world of kendo and the use of the sword. In this text, entitled *Fudochi-shinmyoroku*, he described the techniques of the master of kendo. The first words of this title, *fu do*, mean "not to move."

But this does not mean to be like a stone, to be stuck, to be tight, to be so hard that one could not be pushed; it means to be free and agile, completely flexible at all times. In that sense the mind is unmoved.

Takuan told his disciple, "You are a master of the sword. You must, then, when you practice, be careful of the following. You must not follow the activity of the sword. You must not follow the activity of your mind. You must not follow the activity of your body. You must not try to win; you must not try to lose. You must open your mind completely." Opening yourself up to the heavens and earth completely, letting go of all the thoughts in your mind, standing in front of your opponent, before he moves, you see it, you move there. Before he acts, you block and move. This is the way of a kendo master, and Takuan Zenji knew this. This mind is not moved by form, by outside activities; wide and clear, in each moment it is renewed. In each moment not allowing consciousness to arise at all: This is the state of mind of the kendo master. This is the state of mind of zazen.

We are always trying to find something by which to help ourselves outside ourselves, to make us feel secure for a while. In the modern world we have learned many techniques for gathering information and knowledge. We think it is our responsibility to learn these things; learning *this* and gathering *that* makes us feel that we have done our job in the world. But doesn't our insecurity continue? All of the technology, all of the information, increases day by day, but doesn't our insecurity increase also? Whatever our efforts are, at work and at home, no matter how much we keep learning and how many efforts we keep making, this place of insecurity seems to go on; in fact, it often seems to be growing.

Knowing the not-moving mind—*fudochi*, the mind that is not moving at all, with no knowledge running through it, no thoughts of self, letting go of each thing that comes into our

WORK AND SOCIETY

senses, each thing that comes into our eyes and ears, letting it go, that mind without stain, uncovered and clear—this is our true responsibility. This is what is necessary today. Susokkan is a fine way to work. Mu is a good way to work. Standing, sitting, chanting, eating—from morning until night, from night until morning—we continue until only that final place is left, only the Mu, struggling, continuing, going on, throwing away all self-consciousness, all the things we are caught on, all the shadows, until a vast, expansive state of mind—not only the mind of the zendo but the mind of the Buddha, the mind of Bodhidharma, the mind of all the gods, the mind of the whole universe—is present and sitting with us. This is the point of our practice. This is our responsibility.

Doing Mu we do not work with that word *Mu*. It is the life that manifests that word with which we work. And if we know that place, whether we move our feet or our hands, whether we say "Hello" or "Good morning," it all becomes that Mu. Using all of our senses, completely in vivid training, everything we perceive is Mu. Whether it is the tree in the garden, the garbage bucket, the rake—it all becomes Mu. Thinking about this, feeling that we have done it, is fascination, indulgence, intoxication only. Zen has to be alive, in the present, in every moment and every breath, or it is a waste of precious time.

If we realize this place of no shadow and no small self— that mind with no clutter at all—this is the very source of the countless Buddhas, the original source of all people and the truth of the whole universe. The truth of Buddha and Bodhidharma and all the patriarchs must all be this one Truth. In this Truth there is no birth and no death. If we awaken to our true deep mind, that place where we have no idea of self or attachment to a small self, we will be able to taste the flavor of the Buddha's mind and of Bodhidharma's mind directly. When we can taste that directly we will know that place of no birth and no death from our own experience. And if we can experience that place of no birth and no death for ourselves, then everything that we encounter with our eyes and ears will be seen as the truth itself. We do not see yesterday's flower or moon or stars or sun or tree or mountains or wall or people; we see each thing as it is for the first time.

When we can keep our own egoistic wishes from ruling us, we can then use our wide-open inner eyes to clearly see the suffering and confusion in society. In this way, instead of shutting ourselves up in our own small worlds and setting up boundaries to protect our own selves, we will be able to look wholeheartedly at the confused minds of those in society and know that we must do something to help them, that we must do something to liberate them. We will know that this is our very own problem, and that our problems are society's problems as well. We will be able to see in detail, and we will no longer push aside the problems of society to pursue our own individual wishes. We will then want to work among the people of society, liberating each other. We must put all of our efforts into doing this, vowing deeply within our minds that not a single being will be left behind, all will be liberated through our efforts, and that this work will be done without regret for any of the energy used for it.

In society we cannot stop our work, our jobs, or our lives with our families. To give these things up in order to only practice zazen, to only train, would not be fulfilling the responsibilities that we have taken on in the world. If we take our training this far, until only that which is the consciousness of the whole universe remains, vast and wide, until there is no self, here our responsibility is completely fulfilled. When we let go of all the shadows, when our thoughts are completely cleared away, our true social responsibility is taken care of. When we go to work, we take care of our responsibilities there. At home, with our

WORK AND SOCIETY

family, we take care of our obligations there, too. This work we do with our consciousness, and it is our obligation, but if we are seeing with the eyes of the Buddha, then a whole new way of working and a whole new world will be open to us.

Kobe, January 1995

THE YEAR 1995 BEGAN peacefully. Then, on the morning of the seventeenth of January, in and around the city of Kobe, Japan, there was a severe earthquake, a great shift. At dawn in the chill wintertime, before most people were up and around, in one brief second the earthquake struck. It was experienced by everybody at exactly the same time, happening so suddenly that there was no time for anyone to form any dualistic ideas about it.

At the hour of five-forty in the morning—at Sogenji the morning sutra service had finished and morning sanzen had just begun—there came a violent shaking such as we had never experienced before. Okayama is a full hour from Kobe by the bullet train, yet even so, this violent tremor, which continued over and over and over again, this great shaking, could be felt. The vibration was so strong it seemed as if all the buildings would surely be destroyed. Fortunately, the area around Okayama was mostly undamaged; the earthquake had no great effect in this area.

In the morning news the disaster did not seem to be so enormous, but by the time the evening news was broadcast it was clear what a terrible crisis this was. With each report the news was worse and worse as more and more devastation became apparent. More than four thousand people had died. There were twenty-three people training at Sogenji at this time. They had come from all over the world, and they continued their daily zazen practice. The next morning, however, no one was able to just sit still comfortably, knowing of the suffering in

Kobe. So for the people who had gone through so much in the disaster, for the dead and for those suffering in the aftermath of the earthquake, we chanted a sutra in the morning service in the hondo. Just chanting a vow, however, did not seem sufficient. We wanted also to offer the people of the city of Okayama a chance to realize what we had offered in the sutra service that morning. For this we did takuhatsu in the downtown area of Okayama. On a frost-fallen morning of icy coldness, everyone went out to do takuhatsu with wholehearted energy. We gathered quite a large amount of money and gave it to the local newspaper, which was collecting donations for the victims of the earthquake. We asked that the money be used where it was most needed.

As the news of the earthquake spread around the world, the families, friends, and acquaintances of the people training at Sogenji began calling and sending faxes. The depth with which everyone expressed their concern and caring was very moving. We deeply appreciated all of these expressions of concern and support. People who knew how close Kobe and Okayama are were worried that there might have been some damage at Sogenji; fortunately, there was no damage.

The next morning, the third day after the earthquake—because we were in the middle of sesshin—everyone continued with their zazen. But with the deep karmic connection I have with Kobe, I felt that there must be something more that could be done to help. We decided to go to Shofukuji monastery, where I had trained, and to other temples in the demolished city to see how our friends there were doing and what we could do to help. We filled two cars with as much food as possible—vegetables, bread, cheese, butter, and other supplies—and sought whatever advice was available on how to enter the disaster area. Because regular cars were not being allowed into the city and its surrounding area, we applied to the Prefectural government and

KOBE, JANUARY 1995

received special permission and stickers designating our cars as emergency supply vehicles. With this preparation complete, we left for Kobe. There were many police barriers, but we were able to pass through them easily with special permission.

When we saw what remained of the areas where the earthquake had actually struck, we became physically ill. One could only wonder at how violently the city had been shaken to be so completely and totally destroyed. At the temple of Shofukuji, which stands on a stone foundation at the foot of the mountain, the mountain gate had been destroyed, and tiles from the great roof of the hondo had fallen off in large numbers. For even such a sturdy and solidly built building to be so shaken, it had to have been an excessive, intense shock.

The monks were very grateful for the vegetables and supplies, and just as one would expect of them as monks in training they were continuing with their daily samu, along with their zazen. They were working on cleaning up the debris and destruction throughout the surrounding areas.

There were mountains of rubble everywhere, making it barely possible for a car to get through. As we wended our way to where the earthquake had hit the hardest, we saw large homes and eight-story buildings that had been leveled—flattened without even a shadow remaining. The destruction was worse than that from the bombing of war. The original Japanese building material was wood, although recently other materials are more frequently used. While many of the newer buildings had not budged, the older wooden buildings had become piles of garbage, mountains of debris. I was thinking that even in Japan—this country of earthquakes—this was the worst earthquake ever. Thanks to science and modern technology some buildings did not budge an inch, but four thousand people had still died, and it was said that they were the people who lived in the wooden homes that were so easily destroyed. Most were still in their futons when they died. Then, too, the majority of those who died in the earthquake were the elderly. Most of their houses had been built without foundations, as had always been the practice, so that the houses were just sitting on the ground. In this kind of extreme earthquake it was as if the buildings were raised up into the air and then smashed down to the earth.

An acquaintance of mine whose disciple is training with us at Sogenji is a priest in Kobe. After the war he rebuilt a temple little by little from inexpensive wood. While teaching school he put all of his salary into rebuilding the temple. He also used all of his pension fund, encouraging the members of his congregation to support the building of the temple with their donations. He had rebuilt a fine hondo and other temple buildings, and the work was truly splendid. This seventy-plus-year-old priest often said, "This is my life's work. Thankfully my vow has been fulfilled, and today I am so lucky to have been able to see it completed in this way." When we went to visit this temple only the roof was still up. That huge building was this man's life's work, and it had all been wasted and come to nothing in a matter of seconds. How pitiful and how sad. The hondo was still standing, but the buildings around it had been completely destroyed, and another temple nearby had also been demolished. Roofs had fallen, and posts and beams were overturned and broken and fallen down. All that remained were mountains of rubble.

There was no electricity in the city, no water, no food, and many people had no clothing or place to live. Shelter was provided in the local schools or public halls that were still standing, but there was no familiar home for the people to return to. We saw people dragging posts and beams that could no longer be used for building and using them to make fires to keep warm; seeing these adults and their vacant faces was enough to make one feel the tragedy directly. In this earthquake-prone country, is

KOBE, JANUARY 1995

this one of the given destinies of the people?

What has been the progress of Japan as we look at it fifty years after the Second World War? This is also something I thought about. In the new era we have seemingly made progress in superficial form, but in this one instant of the earthquake that superficial form was destroyed, demolished. This is how it seems now. How transient. As the ancients said, "Things of the world are transient and passing, only that clear mind is of true meaning." What should we hold as our goal and our refuge in life? In today's world where is that something in which we can take refuge, and in which we can find meaning?

Originally, religion was for the purpose of enabling us to realize the True Source of the human mind. Today, religion is formalized and ritualized, like a school education; what should be clarification of our True Source is now only a collecting and selling of information. So we have to ask, what should we be learning and discovering and understanding? What happens to us, finally? At the end of this life, how is it? This True Essence has become vague and unclear, and this is our mind's greatest loss of integrity. I think this is also today's greatest problem.

We currently have a culture making rapid progress in technology and great strides in material development. The scholastic and academic aspects of life have also been deeply researched with the achievement of high levels of understanding. Still, we have lost track of that very source, the actual root of it all, and when it comes to this kind of massive, total destruction, all of our possibilities for refuge suddenly disappear. And this is true not only in a great catastrophe like this violent earthquake. If we look at the conditions in the rest of the world today—in Bosnia, in Sarajevo, in Rwanda, and elsewhere in Africa—all over the world we can find conflict and disaster, back to back. Within these circumstances people are without refuge. With a murky, melancholy, and hopeless state of mind they can

THE PATH TO BODHIDHARMA

find little hope for a bright future or a positive world, only a sad and lonely life. The state of mind of that seventy-year-old priest from that rebuilt temple was probably one of not wanting to do anything at all. All the fruits of his efforts had vanished before his very eyes.

During the war, those who were able to stay alive watched their homes and warm hearths abruptly vanish. They were suddenly parted from beloved family members. Of course they could no longer believe or trust in anything then, either.

In the old days in China there was a priest named Master Tozan. A monk asked him, "How can we escape from this severe heat and cold?" This is not just a question about severe heat and cold. It is a question about the very reality we are always facing—a melancholy and difficult reality, a reality that is full of suffering. People are sick and in pain; people have lost their homes in disasters and wars and have nothing in which to believe any longer and are suffering in their despair. For those whose belongings have all been destroyed, their refuge in the material world has been shown to be empty and meaningless. This kind of pain is always occurring all around us.

Master Tozan answered the monk, "You have to go where there is no hot and no cold!"

The monk continued, "Where is that place where there is no hot or cold? Where is that true place of refuge for the mind?"

The priest answered, "When it is hot, become that heat completely! When it is cold, become one with that cold—completely and totally! When it is painful, become that pain completely and totally, and when you are miserable become that misery totally and completely! In the very midst of that, go beyond all of the thoughts you hold in your mind, let go of all ideas of good or bad or gain or loss—let go of all of these thoughts—and from there grasp that place of your very own vivid life energy! That which directly experiences that 'ouch'—feel that life energy directly, grasp the life energy that feels that pain and sorrow." More important than finding a way out of pain and suffering, or trying to find a place where there is no pain or suffering, is to go directly to that place where the pain and suffering are being experienced, to go to where you feel that pain and that sadness directly and totally. Touch that life energy directly and with your own experience. Use that actual direct experience which you have grasped as your base, and stand up strong and firm. This is how the master answered the monk.

In the Japan of today, with its technological progress, the children have been taken over by computer games, losing all sense of how to enjoy themselves from within. In this time of crisis in Kobe, when the father had lost his place of work and the mother had no kitchen in which to prepare meals, with vacant expressions they made a fire with debris wood to keep warm under the chilly winter sky. With nothing but a small, warming fire, they sat near it. The mother and father who had always been too busy and had had to turn their backs on their children were now nearby, and the children were enjoying this and playing wholeheartedly and with abandon in close proximity. For them there was joy on that day, because they could be close to their mother and father. Of course, they were sorry to have lost their computer games and their own rooms, but they had all survived and their mother and father were there beside them, and that meant more than any object or toy to them. The sorrow of having lost their things had been largely replaced by the joy of their parents' presence. To see the children around those adults, happily lost in their playing, was a reminder of the joy of the moment. The children had actually grasped this idea and were giving life to each moment. We all own and have things, and that's fine, but even without a house, or food, or things, or with just a few old clothes, if we can be directly in touch with what it means to be alive, then there is nothing stronger. It is when we look for something perfect and complete outside ourselves that our life becomes busy and crowded and meaningless, and our inner world becomes diluted and flat.

In the midst of seeing this catastrophe I felt that I had to return to Kobe again and again, to join with the people there in cleaning up after this great ordeal and to give them, even a little at a time, the help to start over again—to begin again and return to their life energy. I pray that they will be able to awaken to this new awareness. Buddhism is not something special. It is just being able to feel things directly with our own life energy.

In modern times Shiki Masaoka brought back to life the Japanese poetry style of haiku. He practiced a lot of zazen and was thoroughly acquainted with the world of Zen. In his later years, when he was seriously ill with tuberculosis, his whole body was in great pain, and he lived in great misery as his body filled with pus and phlegm. He left behind poems written about that time in his life. Shiki Masaoka wrote from his own experience, saying that he had always thought that Zen was something that would enable you to die laughing, but as he was struggling with the pain of his illness he finally realized that this way of looking at things had been a mistake. In Zen, no matter how difficult a time of suffering we may be going through, we dig in and go through the experiencing of it. This is how he had come to see it. This is Shiki Masaoka's own experience and deep understanding, directly grasped and then expressed in a poem:

> *The gourd plant is blossoming;*
> *the phlegm is stuck, caught.*
> *Is this the Buddha?*

Shiki Masaoka, in the midst of his pain, lived it to the end. This way of doing it was his Zen. This is not something to be understood or not understood. All people who live, every one of us, will experience our mind's True Origin. Not limited by the name of God or Buddha, our actual life energy and the way we realize it and live our lives is the true religion.

For those who have lived through this or any other catastrophe, and for those who are in great pain right now, from within that experience use your tanden as the very base for everything throughout the heavens and earth. With both hands stretched outward, experience the joy of being alive! In this is Zen—the true quality of being human and alive. I pray for everyone's most excellent quality of life.

Questions and Answers

Q. HOW IN ZEN training can you be touched by life? How do you gain that tender heart of compassion?

People who seriously enter Zen training are all aiming toward a particular goal, the future possibility of enlightenment. They have felt a need to do something in the world, and they want to learn how to go about doing it. So people who are trying to be compassionate, trying to be in the moment, trying to be loving, trying to be in the present without looking for something outside themselves come to Zen training because they have felt the need to be able to develop in a certain way. They have found that their ability to feel love and compassion has been frustrated because they do not know that source of the mind that allows one to fully express these things. Zen teaching aims toward that particular goal of reaching enlightenment, assuming that those working toward that goal have already felt the desire for the heart of compassion.

People come to Sogenji to go one step further in the development of those qualities of love and compassion. Having already felt those things as necessary but not knowing how to go about expressing them, they come for the particular kind of teaching that I offer. They want those things, but no matter how much they have tried, they have not been able to find them. Now, what about that experience of the mind, where these things are supposed to come from. How can you have a direct encounter with that place when you do not know what it is or how to express it? It is like having an itch on your foot but being able to scratch only the outside of your shoe. What do you do when you want to be more compassionate, when you want to be here in the present, when you want to be able to express that tenderheartedness you feel, but you just cannot do it? How do you go about learning how?

What I teach is that which I know from direct experience, that which I know the way to realizing. People reach a point in their efforts to directly encounter the Original Mind where they feel the need for more ki training, more energy training. They try to be compassionate, but they find that is not so easy because their ego gets in the way, or they try to be in the moment, but there is something preventing them from being able to live in that way. To be able to work on the things that make it difficult for us to experience that true compassion, we have the agenda at Sogenji, what I have learned and am teaching there in specifics.

Thich Nhat Hanh and the Dalai Lama, for example, often talk in terms of compassion when they address large groups of people who need constant reminding, as do the people at Sogenji, that we need to be compassionate, we need to be present, and we need to work from the heart. This is what we are all working toward, and working for. But I am pretty sure that when the Dalai Lama and Thich Nhat Hanh are talking with their own monks, they teach them more specifically and in a more severe, direct way. Their approach to people in general, to those who are looking for an open way to go about living their lives and learning about these inner practices, is to present the need for compassion as one of the most important basics.

Yet when push comes to shove, when you just do not know how to go about realizing the place where this compassion, this heart, this presence comes from, then you need a more severe kind of tool, and that is what Zen training offers, what these teachings are about. One monk who was deeply training at

QUESTIONS AND ANSWERS

Sogenji left to care for a friend who was dying of AIDS. After this friend died, the monk stayed to help another AIDS patient, and then another. His third AIDS patient went completely crazy—he actually had to be taken to a mental hospital. The monk could not handle it. He had had all of this training, and all of this preparation, and yet he found himself in a situation where he could not hold on to that Mu, that center. Because he realized he had not trained enough, he had not dug in far enough to develop fully that compassion, heart, and presence, he returned to do sesshin, just to regain a little bit of that essence of training. He had worked so hard for the three years he was at Sogenji, yet he had not been able to dig deep enough to know the place that would have supplied those things when he needed them the most.

Q. BUT HOW DOES that ki and energy of Zen training all of a sudden open into compassion?

The place where this becomes a problem is in the difference between people who have understood what kensho is—and I am not saying who have actually experienced it—and those who think it is some rainbow-colored supernatural experience. People tend to take all of these words—*enlightenment, compassion, love, tender heart of sadness*—into their brains and conceptualize them. So instead of realizing what it is they are actually feeling, they lay another expression on the situation, thinking that is what they should be feeling. They think they should be loving—therefore they will be loving, no matter what they are actually feeling. They may be angry and furious, but they will try to be loving, because they know they should be loving. Even if they are not feeling compassionate, they will say, "I should be compassionate, so I will try to be compassionate."

But unless your love and compassion arise naturally from a clarified state of mind, you are only repressing a state of mind that is the opposite of what you are making yourself feel. Eventually you are going to suffer the consequences for this. The feelings that are being repressed are merely being camouflaged by those feelings you think you should feel; they will not go away just because it is the popular conception that love, tenderheartedness, and compassion are the emotions to have. That is why this experience of the clear mind is so important. When the clear mind is realized, when these feelings of love and compassion come forth truly, naturally, and spontaneously out of a clear mind, then they are not something that is chosen. Love rather than hate, compassion rather than narrow-mindedness, will evolve naturally from a state of clarity, which brings forth the wisdom to express those things, in the moment. With that experience of a clear mind, there will not be even a thought about whether this is compassion, whether this is love, whether this is tenderheartedness. That clarified mind, from which these things come forth naturally, must be realized and reached before we can begin expressing those emotions truly.

It is frequently the case that even while people are expressing what they imagine to be compassion, even while they are doing what they imagine to be the right thing, at the same time they are ignoring and repressing other feelings that they think they should not have. The monk working with AIDS patients says that when people who are terminally ill are nearing the end of their lives, those helping them are the ones to whom they are the meanest and the nastiest. The people who are giving the patients the most, the ones to whom we think the sufferers should be able to express their true love, are hit by them, threatened by them, so angry and frustrated do the terminally ill become at their own inability to control their lives. It is in such ways that all of these repressed feelings will eventually manifest themselves.

QUESTIONS AND ANSWERS

Unless you realize this clarified place, you will be acting from a conception of what compassion is rather than from true compassion. So, again, we come back to what people need to know: How do you go about realizing the clear mind that is within all of us? It has to be truly encountered and expressed all of the time, not just in one experience that solves your problems for the rest of your life, but by knowing where to return to, how you can reach that clarified mind. Then, as constantly as you are able, you can stay in that clear mind, capable of naturally expressing a true compassion.

That is why, when I teach, I am addressing people who have realized that this training is not about a dualistic idea of "being compassionate or not being compassionate," but about going to that place where there is not even a dualistic sense of "I am now compassionate" or "I am now not compassionate," of reaching the place from which that state of mind comes forth of its own.

Q. WHAT IS THE ZEN definition of suffering? How can I as a nurse help someone who is suffering?

Suffering can be divided into physical suffering and psychological suffering. Physical suffering can be described and defined with medical terms, but psychological suffering cannot be because it is subjective and different for each person. Caregivers can listen to someone talk about his or her suffering, but they cannot know that suffering for themselves because, depending on the person, the description of pain and suffering can be so different for each of us.

From the origin—in the Buddha Nature or clear mind—there is no such thing as suffering. The mirror that reflects the flames of a fire does not get hot. Our Original Mind is just like that. Like a clear mirror it does not experience any pain or emotion; it only reflects it back. The mirror is always clear. Those people who understand this and experience pain from the point of view of its being a "divine grace," or who hold some other internal view that relieves their suffering, are close to the experience of the clear heart, and their experience of pain is much less severe. They are closer to that mirror state—but this, of course, is something that cannot be measured, in the same way that you cannot measure the beauty of a flower.

What is important, however, and what connects the experience of the nurse and that of the patient, is the matter of subjective opinion. A person who sees a flower and can think only about its red color is seeing only one side of the flower, thinking of it as a red thing and not seeing its other aspects. When we listen to a person, if we are not "zero" ourselves we hear according to our own opinions rather than truly listening to what the other person is saying. If, as the patient, we speak from the experience of the pain and are not in a clear-minded state, then we will experience that physical pain as suffering.

The only way to truly alleviate suffering is to help the person realize that source from which all things—including suffering—arise. Any other ways of relieving suffering, with medications or material gifts, are just stopgaps and will not provide true relief. The only way to provide actual relief is to allow a person to be able to clarify and realize directly that source from which the suffering comes—to realize that which is prior to the suffering. That which brings us closer to that original source, that which enables us to realize it, is what is necessary to really see the suffering and know its root and therein its relief.

Q. HOW WOULD YOU define spiritual caregiving?

The whole point of spiritual caregiving is that you cannot give it. What you can do—for yourself and for the other person—is to take away as much as possible. But there is nothing that can be given. When everything is taken away that the per-

QUESTIONS AND ANSWERS

son is caught on, then he or she is closest to zero and the clear mind; the pain is no longer held on to, and neither is the person attached to things that bring pain and suffering with them. So to spiritually give is to be able to take away everything that keeps a person (whether oneself or another) from being zero, from being empty—whatever that is.

Q. IN THIS WORLD that is looking for the extraordinary, for advances in every area, how do we be extraordinary in Zen?

The idea of the extraordinary comes from the American dream. We are at a time in the history of human beings when people can choose among an enormous range of possibilities when deciding how to live their lives. They think about what they would like, and they believe that once they have obtained enough material possessions, their lives will be without problems. In fact, this is a time of great problems in terms of our state of mind, because people have come to see enlightenment as just one more thing to be obtained. They decide that they want this particular part of what is called Zen without knowing the means to go about realizing it.

The teachings of the Buddha have an amazing width and breadth. From his very first teachings to his very last, he was offering expedient means for all varieties of people to be able to realize the ultimate part of the path. People were looking at many different ways to go about gaining the experience that the Buddha had.

In the same way, there are those today who have understood that enlightenment is not something extraordinary, who have seen that there is a long process involved. But there are also people who have just seen this excellent little framed jewel of an experience and said, "I want that, please." They think enlightenment is some extraordinary thing, and they want the results of the process without looking at what it takes to realize the process itself. This must be seen as a problem, when just that one aspect is looked at as opposed to the whole of the training.

In the world today there are people who do not have the wherewithal even to be able to read about enlightenment in books. If you ask people in many parts of the world what they want more than anything else, they will say, "I want a potato and cabbage for my soup tomorrow." What you would teach them about their state of mind is quite different from what you would teach a person who has read the whole of the *Lotus Sutra* and said, "I want this wonderful experience."

That is why the Buddha's teachings cover such a broad expanse. In the *Lotus Sutra* he was saying, "Accept everything, accept even your difficult places, accept all of it." For someone who already has a satisfying life, and all the material comforts one needs, that may be possible. Even so, the idea of accepting everything all too often becomes a conceptual understanding of acceptance only—so that one ends up gritting one's teeth and saying, "I accept this, I accept this." Yet even when we are not yet able to have the state of mind that actually accepts everything, at least we may know we need to move toward it.

Those people who want a potato for tomorrow's soup could not care less about accepting anything that comes along, or about the question of what their state of mind is—all they want is a potato. They have no interest whatsoever in understanding their mind. The spiritual needs of the people on this planet vary widely. If we look at the people of America or of the West who have satisfied their material needs, what is their greatest problem? It is a problem of their state of mind. Now that they have satisfied their physical needs, how do they go about satisfying the spiritual needs?

When one reads about enlightenment but is not actually going through the process of experiencing it, one cannot understand what the process takes and what is required. But the first step is to know that one actually wants to do this; then one can learn what needs to be done to go about experiencing it for oneself. At first, everyone will do it in a dualistic way, saying, "I'm going to become compassionate," and then acting in terms of what they think compassion is; saying, "I'm going to become loving," and then acting in terms of what they think being loving is. When you do that, you find it does not work. So this kind of misguided curiosity becomes a guided curiosity, taking you along to the place where you truly can understand the teachings of the Buddha.

This whole thing has to be seen as a spectrum of needs for different people. You cannot teach people who are just beginning about these extraordinary things without also teaching the whole process that leads to their realization. By wanting these things, but not knowing what they have to go through to realize them, they actually begin to follow the Path.

Q. WHEN SOMEBODY REALIZES their Buddha Nature, that clear mind, is that the same thing as realizing what might be called Christ consciousness in Christianity? Do all of the different spiritual traditions serve as inductions to the same higher place, or do they serve as inductions to different higher places?

The word that is used in Buddhism is *Dharma*. The way the universe works is that that which is prior to all of our ideas of things is something that only reflects back, that cannot itself be reflected. This is the state of mind we speak of as realizing your Buddha Nature, or your Christ consciousness, for example. Because of the nature of that place, all of these experiences have to be the same. There is only one truth. There is only one particular experience, and when you are within that place of clear-seeing, in that place that reflects back but cannot be seen, because that place has no differentiation and no dualism, there cannot be any such differences as those between religious names or religious descriptions. That experience is the same in every single religion, and in every case the experience is beyond description. That experience beyond description, that experience that cannot be explained in a way that is particular to any one religion's expression of it, is the essence that is the same in each religion.

Without a canvas there cannot be a painting, and without a screen a film cannot be shown. But that canvas on which there is no painting, that screen on which nothing is being shown, or that chalkboard on which nothing is written—that is the state of mind we are talking about here. Once something is named, expressed, described, it is like putting paint on a canvas, or projecting a film on the screen, or writing words on the chalkboard. What we are talking about is all prior to that.

When you are in that state of mind, whatever you want to name it after you have experienced it, there is no possibility of an awareness of a descriptive way to look at it, because everything is without a dualistic sense at that time. There are tools that can be described—for example, prayer or susokkan or koan work—and those tools are part of a process that leads to that state of mind, but when that state of mind is reached, then even though we have a physical body we are no longer aware of any sense of it. We may be sitting in a room, but we are no longer aware of our surroundings. We have lost track of all those distinctions and dualistic ways of looking at things. It is not that they do not exist in some sense, but what is being aware is the mind that has been described as being like a mirror, the mind that reflects back but is empty of anything itself, the mind of zero. These are all, again, descriptions, but this is what is being talked about as that basic bottom line in which there is no sense of any dualistic perception of things as relative to each other.

QUESTIONS AND ANSWERS

Q. BUT IF I HAVE LOST track of the room and of my body, how am I supposed to walk around during the day? How do I do my job if I have made my mind empty of all awareness? How do I participate in my life in this state of mind?

It is not like that exactly. This is something that is very difficult to understand with the rational mind, but it is something I am asked about all the time. What I have described is true of that actual encountering of the Buddha Nature or the Christ consciousness, which then leads us to be able to let go of that attachment to an ego. When we experience the essence of this Buddha Nature, when we see that we are this clear mind, then we are in fact able much more easily to move through our day. When we experience this place in which we are free from any egoistic delusion, we do not all of a sudden lose all of our previous experience. We still have our brain cells, and we retain all of the things we have learned; in that sense we do not become babies that are like blank slates. Everything we have learned, everything we know, everything we have experienced is still available to us, but we now have the choice of whether or not we want to view the world through an egoistic filter. In talking about this, we can use the analogy of a lens, which can be cleaned when it becomes dirty. When we know that we have a clear vision, we can still use our ego, but at the same time we can also choose to be free from it. Because we are no longer attached to it, we can use it appropriately. We can also be free to experience things directly without that attachment to a small self, without the intellectualized, egoistic filter through which we so often view things.

In the same way, people frequently ask, "If you are looking at things in that way, if you have gotten rid of your self, then isn't it hard to know how to go about doing the things you need to do to live in the world?" In fact, quite the opposite is true. When one is no longer attached to and concerned with the small self, one realizes from the same place that we realize the Buddha Nature or the Christ consciousness that something else is living through us that is able to function. When the ego is affixed to something we see only a very narrow view; when that something is let go of, a greater wisdom, a greater awareness, a greater ability to function is able to live through us and be present at each and every moment. It takes time to learn how to let go of that ego, but once we have experienced that place of freedom from it, we feel less threatened by the prospect of letting go of it and allowing that greater awareness to work through our lives. When we can let go of that ego at any given moment, rather than being left without the ability to function, we are full of a much greater wisdom. We are able to move and act and behave in a richer way because we are no longer caught by some idea of how things should be. This emptiness is not something that you can conceptualize; it is a state of being empty of ego, but of being full of what can come through when that ego has been let go of.

Q. IS THERE SUCH A THING as reincarnation or transmigration of souls?

Buddhism is not a religion with an outside power. In a religion with an outside power you are guaranteed that you will go to heaven in the next life if you follow the guidance of God, the Absolute, or go to hell if you do not. Buddhism does not have this heaven and hell. It attributes creation of things not to a god but to cause and effect. Everything has a cause. Wherever you go, whatever difficulties you face, there is a cause for it. Through these causes, karmic connections are formed. Due to various causes your mother and father had the karmic connection to get married, and from this source came your own birth. There is no relation to a god here.

From the point of view of science, life was born on this planet several billion years ago; about one million years ago, through the course of a long journey, humankind as we know it was born from that life. Since then human life has continually been reproducing new life up to the present day. That is the scientific view; although science is not the same as Buddhism, this view also proceeds from cause to effect. Everything manifests because of cause and effect. Nothing is brought forth by a god. If you believe that God determines your next life, choosing who goes to heaven and who goes to hell, then it becomes God's decision.

This idea of reincarnation and the problem of a next life arise in people's minds when they ask about what they see in this present life: Why is this person that way? How can that person be so awful? When you start to think about it, it seems that each person's personality must come from something they have done in the past or in some other life. This is natural. This person is born to a rich family, that one to a poor family. This person is intelligent, that one is foolish. There are many such things we can see. Everybody wants to be the one born in the rich family and to be happy; nobody wants to be the unlucky one. So when you analyze it, you come to the conclusion that it is because of past difficulties that one is born into difficult circumstances. When we look at our ancestors, things seem to have been handed down from each parent to the next child for many generations, so it is natural to assume the existence of that kind of cause and effect from past lives. There is nothing mysterious about that. Also, it is natural to think that because there seems to be a future, there must also have been a past, and vice versa. We live in this natural flow of life continuously appearing.

That is not to say that there is anything like a soul. When we think in terms of this one individual body, we all know that it will die. It is clear to everyone that everything that is born will die. In Buddhism we are not talking about a tiny little soul and whether it is going to be born in another body. We are viewing life from the vast flow of life itself. If you look at life from this larger perspective, everyone has the same life. Everyone is part of that same vast power. One form dies away, but the universal life keeps moving.

Being born, existing, being destroyed, dying, and then being born anew, this is how it works: Life is one great wave of universal existence, a vast continuous flow of life, not just one small individual physical body. The mind has only a tiny pinhole view of this overall flow. When it asks "Will I be born as a pig or a monkey next time?" it is thinking in terms of a separate form, of being reincarnated in another small separate form. It is not like that. The difference between a pig and a monkey is irrelevant within this immense universal flow. Everything is a part of the same life, and those specific forms are just concrete manifestations of that larger flow.

We often hear in Buddhism about that wheel of death and birth. In fact, this was already a teaching being given in India before the birth of the Buddha. When we talk about this wheel, what is being referred to is this continuing flow of life. In ancient India, this wheel of birth and death had six different stages that continually followed each other in a cycle, repeating themselves. These six worlds or stages were the realm of hell, the realm of the hungry ghosts, the realm of the angry gods, the realm of the animals, the realm of humans, and the realm of the heavenly beings.

We hear especially in Tibetan Buddhism about reincarnation, about the cycle of rebirth, and about these six realms, and we often wonder how this works and what it means. But what I think the Buddha was teaching was that it is only a matter of whether in every single moment we are functioning from that clear mind or not. This clear mind is not something that we must wait until our next life to be able to experience, depending on how we live this life; whether we live every moment from this awakened state of mind or whether we cloud it over is what the Buddha was talking about. It is not taught any place in the sutras that we will have a next life; these six realms are not something that we will experience when we are reborn in another life. They could apply to different parts of society; they could apply to different aspects of our current life; they could apply to our various states of mind.

People often think: "I can't believe what this person says"; "I can't trust this person who is sitting next to me"; "I can't believe in this person who lives next door to me"; "I can't really trust that person down the street, I really don't believe what they say"—there is no hell more horrible than not being able to believe in our fellow human beings or even in people whom we know well. And then there are times when, without knowing why, we become irritated and upset and angry, when for no reason at all deep feelings of irritation arise and we hurt someone's feelings and make them feel bad, with no control over what we are doing—these are the feelings of the angry guardians. Sometimes, even though we have everything we need, even though we have had enough to eat, we want more, we just have to have more; we are not really hungry, we do not really need anything, we just want more—this kind of greediness is the realm of the hungry ghosts. Sometimes we do something about which we are so embarrassed, about which we become so deeply ashamed, that we are unable to tell anybody about it—this is the world of the animals. Sometimes we truly reflect on and regret the things we have done, reviewing our behavior and working to change ourselves, thinking, "I just really should not have done that" or "I wish I had not said that"—this is the world of humans. And sometimes we forget ourselves completely while enjoying the pleasures of music, or sports, or some wonderful pastime in which we are so happy that we become absorbed in it totally—this is the world of heavenly beings.

When one sees clearly into one's own mind, one sees that the worlds of the hell beings, the hungry ghosts, the angry gods, the animals, humans, and heavenly beings are all based within oneself—that we are the vehicle. But the self-conscious ego is very heavy and is always pushing us to the right and to the left. It is easy to believe that when this small ego dies, this self-conscious self, then there will be nothing more, that life will end. But such a way of seeing things is just not accurate.

Nothing will truly disappear; nothing real will die. The flow of the universe just as it is, vast and infinite—this continuity is the substance of our true body. From our own experience of clarity and serenity we can recognize this as ourselves. Of course, the self-conscious ego manifests in many different forms, one after the other. These, however, are all contained in and moving within the great womb of the universe. In reality there is not even an actual ego to be reborn. It is because people think there is a separate self that they believe in reincarnation. They think they are moving through these different worlds of the animals, humans, heavenly beings, and so on. But the universal self is not such a tiny limited thing. It is vast spaciousness, infinite expansiveness—this is what we are!

All the problems we find in society arise because people believe in the actual existence of this separate self. The idea of rebirth is a tool for helping us to let go of this concept of a separate self. It can be used for liberating people from this limited conception of life rather than for creating worry about what will happen in the future or as an excuse for not taking responsibility for one's present life condition.

You can spend a lot of time thinking about why this happened and why that person is that way, but that is useless and has nothing to do with Buddhism. Rather, the idea of rebirth can be used to teach us to let go of our limitations in this present life—not in order to have a better life the next time around but as a way of seeing that the concept of life itself as a small separate ego with all these troubles has nothing to do with the vast spaciousness of the flow of the universe. Calculating and worrying about problems and what kind of family you might be born into is all deluded and self-centered concern that can last only for the space of this lifetime. Within the vastness and immensity of the universe it is all the same. From that vast spaciousness life is born within that great life. It is obvious that individual forms do come forth and die away, but we do not live in our own small world. Rather, we live within the circulating energy of all of humanity.

Buddhism demands that you go beyond such limiting concepts as thinking that your small self alone is the universe. It is only one bit of the scenery. Wake up to this rich expansiveness, this bounteous flow—the world of zazen! When you let go of that tiny separate self-concept you will be able for the first time to know the small self as one of the manifestations of the entire universe—only one bit of the scenery. By letting go of this concept of a separate self and allowing all extraneous things to drop away, you can for the first time understand this individual physical self as the immensity and expansiveness of the universe itself. You can know there is no birth and no death.

When I say that there is no birth and no death I do not mean that there is no physical birth and no physical death, but rather that living and dying take place within the flow of the universe. We can understand this state of mind through our own experience and have no fear. This does not mean that we will lose all fear of dying or that we will not feel lonely at being separated from those who have died; rather, it means that, although we are separated, we know we will meet again in some form. We will meet in a different way, thus realizing reunion in the grand sense.

THE PATH TO BODHIDHARMA

Q. THE BUDDHA TEACHES that everyone is equal, that we are all already perfect just as we are, yet the way of life of the monastery is built on a fairly rigid system of hierarchy. How can you explain that?

One has to be careful to look at this question of equality from the point of view of its essence, not from the point of view of its form—that is, in terms of an inner equality rather than in terms of an outer appearance or external approach to equality. When we look at the idea of equality from the point of view of outer appearances or material possessions, we end up with something like communism, where everything is judged in terms of its equality in a material sense. In fact, even when by outward appearances all of the material factors seem to be equal, the inner part of it, people's minds and inner workings, will never actually be equal. It is not possible for people in a physical sense ever to be totally equal.

What the Buddha was teaching was an equality of the clear nature in all people, that which is within all of those external, physical differences. If we try to apply this concept in an external rather than an internal context, we end up with what in Japanese is called "poison equality," where things appear to be treated with equality, but in fact that is not what is going on. From the outside it might seem that people are being treated equally, but their inner essence, the way they function inwardly, is not being given consideration.

What the Buddha was talking about was being able to see that all things are equal from the inside and that all of us have the same Buddha Nature—that no matter how we appear to be from the outside, there is a part of all of us that is exactly the same. The monastery attempts to put into action what the Buddha taught, to function in terms of the very excellent way of looking at this that the Buddha had. The "poison equality," in which things are superficially looked at as equal but in fact are

QUESTIONS AND ANSWERS

inwardly not at all equal, can be avoided by having the person who has, for even one second or one day, moved in the direction of clarifying his or her true nature be considered a senior. The person who was even one moment ahead of someone else, not considering age or anything else, would be the one who was the senior, and the people who came after that person would be the juniors—that is how this hierarchy of the monastery was born.

Unfortunately, we do not all have the wisdom of the Buddha. Although ideally this is a very good system, problems occur when it comes to putting it into action in a monastery. The people who are participating in this system are still in training, and they are not able to express the same state of mind continually. They start thinking that it is because of their egoistic self that they are first, rather than because of their vow to realize their True Nature. In the monastery one frequently sees examples of people who are able for a moment to reach this way of seeing that the Buddha expressed, but soon they want to protect their position, they want to protect their egoistic personality, and they express their seniority from an egoistic, unclear place and begin bossing people around.

It should be the position of the senior monks sometimes to teach, sometimes to support from below, sometimes to correct, to do many different things to help those who come after them, sharing what they have learned first. But instead, the way they go about doing it becomes egoistic itself, with the senior monks pressing down on those who are below them, unable to treat them in an equal way because their own egos and their own personalities still have not developed to the place where they can do things in the way the Buddha envisioned when he formulated this system in the first place. This happens frequently, even to the extent that a senior monk might become physically violent in his interactions with a junior monk. This is a mistake. This is not right. This is something about which we can only be ashamed. This is not how the system should be used, but it happens because not everyone who is in training is able to maintain this realized state of mind all the time.

It is very difficult for people to know what really is true kindness. One example is the *keisaku*, or the stick used in the zendo. Those who are used to being hit with it are thankful for it and understand the kindness of the keisaku when it is used to help them get rid of thoughts, or wake up, or come out of a drowsy zazen. But those who do not understand will think that those who do zazen using the keisaku are nothing but violent gangsters hitting each other with sticks. In fact, I hear many jokes to that effect. People who do not understand this kindness and how it works could look at the keisaku and legitimately see it as wrong. And that is also true of much behavior in the monastery. With the keisaku, for example, it is taught that what is most important is the mind with which it is given and received; the bowing and the carefulness with which the keisaku is given and received are for the purpose of maintaining a compassionate frame of mind.

We can truly think that we are doing things for other people. Yet over and over, although we intend to act in the right way when we speak to our juniors, when we take care of our sangha and the people around us, we find that even though we are acting with that intention we are unable to keep the ego from influencing our actions because we are not yet all realized people. For that reason, and from the olden days when the Buddha was teaching his sangha, there developed a practice that was still observed until the Middle Ages in Japan, although it is not formally practiced anymore. The word for this practice in Japanese could be translated as "confessional repentance," but it does not have the sense of medieval penitence that comes with the English translation. Rather, the practice is a process of reviewing your behavior, of looking at what you have done and seeing

QUESTIONS AND ANSWERS

whether the ego was involved, whether you were acting with a clear mind. This is not something to do once a year or once a month or once a week; every single day you should review your behavior, truly examining it to see if during that day you were acting from a clear mind or in an ego-driven way.

In the old days, once a year there would be a public ceremony of repentance or reviewing of behavior. In addition, at the end of each of the training periods, there would be an official, formal process of repentance. But the formal process was less important than for each and every member of the sangha to do this daily review of behavior as a practice. As far as I know, this practice is not being done formally anywhere in Japan in Zen training today, but it is a practice that would be helpful—especially to address this very problem of people dealing unskillfully with those who are above or below them. One way to avoid such problems would be for everyone, no matter where they are in the hierarchy, to have the practice of reviewing their behavior to see if their actions are coming from the right state of mind.

There is a specific way of going about this reviewing of behavior. In fact, there is a sutra that goes with it, which uses the word *repentance*—I use that word in English for want of a better translation.

Zange zange rokkon zaisho
Metsu jo bonno metsu jo gosho
Namu Shakamuni Butsu
Zange zange rokkon zaisho
Metsu jo bonno metsu jo gosho
Namu shoso Daruma Daishi
Zange zange rokkon zaisho
Metsu jo bonno metsu jo gosho
Namu sange sanzen shobutsu
Zange zange rokkon zai sho
Metsu jo bonno metsu jo gosho

An easily chantable English translation is:
> *Review! Repent! The stains of the six senses!*
> *Transient, and cut! The selfish desires.*
> *Transient and cut! The ancient twisted karma.*
> *Honor to the Buddha!*
> *Honor to Bodhidharma!*
> *Honor to the infinite Buddhas, past, present,*
> *   and future.*

The start of that sutra could be more fully translated as "Review, repent, with all the roots of the six senses, see deeply into the faults or sins that they have brought forth." As the sutra is chanted, we look carefully at each of the six senses—eyes, ears, nose, tongue, body, mind—in turn. For example, with our tongue we often say things that are not true and arise from an egoistic need. In speaking, even though we may not intend to, we often say things that offend other people. So we look carefully at how we have used our tongue in order to see how our behavior has been manifested. The sixth sense is our mind. Often we intend to do something that is kind, but when that intention comes from an egoistic place we can be deceiving ourselves about how we treat people. We think our actions are going to be clear, but we express ourselves in a way that is far different from what we intended. We end up deceiving not only ourselves but also others when we act from an unclear or deluded state of mind, or when the words we speak reflect our egoistic needs instead of our clear mind.

In the same way we review each of the six senses to see to this meticulous degree how our behavior actually appears to others. Thus the first part of this sutra is "Review! Repent! The stains of the six senses." Then it directs you to cut away desires and cut away deep karma. Finally, you offer "honor to the Buddha," "honor to Bodhidharma," and "honor to the infinite Buddhas, past, present, and future." By repeating this sutra over

QUESTIONS AND ANSWERS

and over and carefully looking into your behavior, you come to a place—it is the same place you reach in zazen—where your mind is completely clear and transparent. You see only the scenery immediately in front of you, with nothing distracting you from that direct perception. This state of mind in itself is samadhi. We often have a difficult time entering this state because we have an idea of what samadhi is and we try to reach for that idea. But, in fact, this repentance or reviewing of behavior is in itself a clarifying zazen and can provide an entrance into this state of absolute attention and clear awareness.

I am often asked why in our busy lives we should take the time to sit zazen—everyone has so much to do, and they think they cannot take time away from their daily activities to just sit. But by taking this time we can in fact clarify what it is we are actually doing during all those busy hours. Zazen is the process of being able to see ourselves. When we attain a stable and well-aligned mind, we can for the first time see clearly what we are doing, and we will no longer make the same mistakes. For that reason, repentance is a very important practice to teach.

People who sit zazen trying to become something, not letting go of the things they are holding on to but trying to obtain or attain a certain state of mind, move further and further away from what this clarifying of mind, this repentance, can do. When we try to find some state of mind that we have experienced before, or we have an idea about what our state of mind should be and strive to attain that goal, our sitting becomes more and more cumbersome; when we cannot find the state of mind we think we should be attaining, the weight of the ego becomes heavier and heavier. This process I am describing—of clarifying our behavior—is a way of emptying rather than of putting on. I try always to bring this into my teaching because people are often unaware of this way of practicing. I feel that much of the behavior that creates problems in the monastery comes from the lack of this type of practice, from people doing their practice without ever reviewing their behavior or looking carefully at how their behavior is reflecting their zazen. We have a great gift from society to be able to spend so much time doing zazen, but our zazen also allows us the opportunity to look at our behavior and clearly see how we are manifesting our practice. If we do not use it for that, we are wasting an excellent chance and will be endlessly doing a form of dead-end, closed-circuit zazen that exists only as an idea of something we think we are trying to pursue. We will never be able to attain a state of clear awareness and function in the world with that actual clear mind.

If you do your zazen, do your sesshin, without also clarifying your actions and reviewing your behavior in the way I have just described, you are never going to find a clear path to awareness and enlightenment and realize your true nature. That is true for everybody. You can practice forever, but without this particular part of it, your practice will not open up into that realization.

The last line of the sutra of repentance talks of honoring all the Buddhas of the past, present, and future. Although the words refer to "the infinite Buddhas," they actually include all things: all the rocks, the stars, the sun, the earth, the water, everything; to all the myriad things, you are also repenting, to everything that exists you bow down and prostrate in repentance and in review of your behavior. I find this a very important practice, and I do it myself every day, particularly at nighttime when I am doing *yaza*, or late-night sitting after the regular bedtime. During the first part of my yaza I do this part of my zazen, and then I find my clear mind to be relieved. Of course, there has to be an intent behind this reviewing of your behavior—it is not just an empty repetitive chanting—but as you do this practice, then from that place of repentance will come this vast wide-open mind, and then you sit in that. For everybody to make a practice of doing this once a day is a very good idea.

QUESTIONS AND ANSWERS

Q. HOW IS IT POSSIBLE to tell a true teacher from a false one?

More than eleven hundred years ago in China, in the ninth century, lived Obaku Zenji. When a monk asked Obaku Zenji this very question, he replied, "All over China there are monasteries full of thousands of monks, and everywhere these monks are asking this question. Why are they just licking the fart gas of the ancients like that? What are they doing taking on the dregs of the remnants of learning in such a way?"

The student asked further, "Are you saying that even though there are thousands of students all over China who are practicing Zen, there is not one single person who is valid among those teaching them?"

To which Obaku answered, "In this forest of many, many Zen monks, there is not one true teacher." What he was saying to this monk is that no matter where you look, to even think you can find a true teacher is an absurd idea.

When the monk continued pressing his question, Obaku said, "There will never be a time when there is no Zen. Zen is always and everywhere, but there is not one true teacher." What he was saying is that this true teacher does not have a specific form. If you believe the priests everywhere who say, "I am a teacher," if you believe there is someone who is actually as enlightened and as deeply awakened as the Buddha, you are making a big mistake. Zen is not about looking outside yourself for that person; it is about finding that teacher where you are and in everything around you. To think in terms of finding a person who is saying "I am a true teacher," "I am deeply enlightened," is a great mistake; what needs to be done is to see the real thing right in front of you.

It is important that we understand the deep kindness of Obaku in answering his monk this way. We spend so much time saying, "Well, this teacher said these words," "That teacher said those words," and "This wonderful thing was said by that person." What a great mistake that is can be seen if we look at the teachings of the Buddha. Never once does the Buddha say, "And this person says" or "And that persons says." The idea that there is something to treasure that is outside ourselves—that is not within our own experience of this true, clear mind—is a mistake. When we look outside ourselves all we find is words and people. That is why Obaku said, "In all this great country of China there is no true master."

That which has to be realized is not something outside ourselves or something that we can understand from someone else's words. It is the experience itself that is valid; that someone else's words have been used to describe the experience is not the point. In fact, this level of awareness is beyond any form, beyond any words, and beyond calling it the teaching of the Buddha. At this point even that form or that personality or that historical personage of the Buddha is no longer necessary. The Buddha himself said to his disciples, at the end of his life, that they should take refuge in nothing outside themselves—he told them to look only into their own clear mind for refuge, only to the Dharma for refuge. Only to these should they look for wisdom and comfort when he was gone. To go beyond all conceptions of a teacher and experience that place where there is no longer any need for or any lingering idea of a Buddha is what Obaku was pointing his student to when he gave him this very kind answer.

It is to this degree that we must realize the True Mind that connects each and every one of us—not the ego, but that clear mind that unites all people and all beings. Please, we must each take responsibility for realizing this truth for ourselves. For the doing of this I offer these words, asking you to taste deeply their flavor.

Glossary

Bankei Yotaku (1622–1693): While Hakuin is famous for having united and gathered the Rinzai line in his time, his flavor of Zen alone could not liberate the non-ordained as well as the ordained. Bankei always taught from his own experience, using words so plain and clear they could guide common people as well as scholars. With no attachments to lineage, sect, or system, he taught "unborn zen," that all people are endowed with the "Unborn Buddha Nature." To realize this is the marrow of zen.

Bodhidharma (d. 532): The twenty-eighth patriarch in line from the Buddha and the first patriarch of Zen. For more on his life and teachings, see the chapter "Bodhidharma's *Outline of Practice*."

Bodhisattva vow: Each and every person is endowed from birth with Buddha Nature. But "Buddha Nature," or "Pure Mind," is only a borrowed name for what cannot be described in words. Buddha Nature is about awakening to the wisdom with which we are originally endowed and then taking that wisdom into society. In this wisdom there are two entwined facets: (1) While always deepening our clear mind, (2) we bring liberation to all beings. We seek truth always and with the light of that truth we return to society to spread and share it. We all already have Buddha Nature from birth; to manifest it is to give life to the Bodhisattva vow. Although it is not possible to know the full light of this wisdom without awakening, compassion is possible in this very moment. That mind of wanting to do anything that one can for the pain of society can be known and acted on in this very moment. To always think of society and offer ourselves completely is our essence and our responsibility. Through the doing of this we will be able to move beyond the things we are caught on and to clarify our minds with the wisdom that arises through functioning. It must work in this way or there can be no true liberation of all beings.

Buddha: See Shakyamuni.

Buddhadharma: See Dharma.

Dharma: In the objective world of material reality there is scientific truth, such as $1 + 1 = 2$. This truth cannot be disproved by anyone. The Dharma, or Buddhadharma, is the law of the Mind that no one can bend. Because the Buddha awakened to these rules they are called the Buddhadharma. But even if the Buddha had not awakened to them, the Dharma would still be the Dharma. As Rinzai says, the True Mind has no form and extends in all ten directions; our mind has no form or substance, yet it extends throughout the universe and embraces all without exception. All people's minds, when they encounter the true root, experience the same essence and realize that we are all embraced in this with no exception. The law of clear mind as defined by the sixth patriarch is: (1) While having a nen (mind moment), not to be caught on any nen. This means having no attachment to anything that we see, hear, taste, or feel. (2) While working and functioning, not to be caught on any external object or event. Forgetting ourselves in our work or activity we encounter objects and people but are not caught on each and every detail. In the same way that water fits into a vessel, we have no separate or fixed idea of who we are. (3) With nothing before birth and nothing after birth, the mind is always new. In this very moment and place the mind is always unhampered, not fixed or moved around. The simple clear mind works like this, and this is Dharma, which cannot be defined in hard, fast words.

Dogen Kigen (1200–1253): Credited with founding the first Zen monastery in Japan, Dogen is best known today as the founder of the Soto school of Zen.

Dojo: Most commonly, *dojo* refers to a place where one can join a teacher and according to his teaching dig deep within and clarify the essence of Zen. In Japan, each Zen training dojo is affiliated with a headquarters temple that is then responsible for it. Nevertheless, as it is written in the *Vimalakirti Sutra*, a dojo is not necessarily a formal location but rather refers to the mind's true clarification of this essence. All people of training can be working to clarify this essence wherever they go; it does not require a system or a prescribed building. Three people and a true teacher supporting and polishing each other are a dojo.

Funyo Zensho (942–1024): The Rinzai Zen master whose Chinese name is Fen-yang Shan-chao.

Ganto Zenkatsu (828–887): The Zen master of the Tang dynasty whose Chinese name is Yen-t'ou Chuan-huo.

Hakuin Ekaku (1685–1768): A Japanese Zen master. For more on his life and teachings, see the chapter "Hakuin and His *Song of Zazen*."

Hannyatara Sonja: Bodhidharma's teacher, the twenty-seventh Indian patriarch. His Sanskrit name is Prajnadhara.

THE PATH TO BODHIDHARMA

Hondo: The traditional layout of a Zen temple had a *butsuden* where the statue of the Buddha was honored, sutras were read, and the footprints of the ancients were studied. In the butsuden, the statue of the Buddha was placed centrally, where prostrations could be made to it. Separately, there was a *hato*, where a teacher with the same awakening experience as the Buddha taught the Dharma. The mountain gate, or main gate of the temple, was in front of these two buildings. Later, the functions of the butsuden and the hato were combined into one building, known as the hondo.

Ikkyu Sojun (1394–1481): This Japanese Zen master taught in a time of extreme political strife, with many changes and upheavals in society. He publicly criticized the religious leaders of his day for being attached to formalization and for being far from essence. He lived among the people in order to truly touch them at their own level. His level of awakening was vast and abundant, and he taught with great humor and wisdom. In his writings, which became very famous, he offered severe criticisms and stressed the essence of the ancients. People welcomed and loved him, and he opened the minds of thousands.

Isan Reiyu (771–853): The Zen master whose Chinese name is Kuei-shan Ling-yu; the teacher of Kyogen Chikan.

Jimyo Insui (986–1039): Also known as Sekiso Soen, his Chinese name is Shih-shuang Ch'u-yuan.

Joshu Jushin (778–897): This Zen master, who lived at the end of the Tang dynasty, is known in Chinese as Chao-chou Ts'ung-shen. He lived so long and so fully that it is said he did twice as much training, twice as much teaching, and lived twice as long as most people. With his subtle and deep flavor he gave us the barrier koan of Mu though which all Zen students must pass. For more on his life, see the chapter "Zazen."

Kalpa: An infinitely long period of time.

Kanji: The Chinese characters that make up a significant portion of the Japanese written language.

Kanzan Egen (1277–1360): The founder of Sogenji's headquarters temple, Myoshinji; he is also known as Muso Daishi, or "Great Teacher Muso."

Kendo: Japanese-style fencing.

Kensho: Enlightenment; the awakening to one's true nature, prior to ego. In our original clear and pure mind there is not a speck of dualism or of any impurity. To awaken to this true original quality of the mind is to experience kensho.

Ki: A universal force that constitutes and moves all things. As we take in food and water and oxygen our energy is deepened, and our common living essence increases. According to the ways of Eastern medicine, one's respiration fills one with ki, and with this living energy one can touch and affect many things. When we do zazen, using our tanden breath, we revitalize not only our own bodies but the people and world around us.

Koan: Specific words and experiences of the ancients that cannot be understood by logic or rational thought. The word *koan* originally referred to a case that established a legal precedent. In Zen, however, a koan is not a case that deals with past and future, good and bad; rather, it allows us to clarify the truth by cutting through all of these concepts. If we cannot pass through the patriarchs' gates, our path will be obstructed by dualistic concepts such as good and bad, past and future; we will be nothing more than a blown weed caught by words describing someone else's experience. And what is this passage of the patriarchs? As it is said in the *Mumonkan*, people who want to clarify this Great Matter must focus on Joshu's Mu with single-minded determination, and then we can not only meet the living Joshu but also can walk hand-in-hand with the ancients, seeing with their eyes and hearing with their ears.

Kyogen Chikan (d. 898): The Zen master whose Chinese name is Hsiang-yen Chih-hsien. For his life story, see the chapter "Hakuin and His *Song of Zazen*."

Mumon: See Yamada Mumon; *Mumonkan*.

Mumonkan: A collection of forty-eight koans compiled by Mumon Ekai (Wu-men Hui-k'ai; 1183–1260). The title is often translated in English as *The Gateless Gate*.

Nansen Fugan (748–835): The Zen master whose Chinese name is Nan-chuan Pu-yuan.

Nen: The mind of right now; a single mind instant without any added associations; that which is brought forth and moves in accordance with the world of this moment but in which there is no past experience or memory or thinking about this or that. Even when our essence is strong, if we are entertaining extraneous thoughts we cannot see things clearly. We use susokkan or koans to focus our minds into a state of oneness. When we encounter each and every thing with no extraneous thinking and with sharp focus, that which is realized is a pure nen. Taking it one step further, if our focus is clear and sharp, when something

GLOSSARY

is over and finished, nothing of it remains or lingers to be dragged along to the next moment.

Niso Eka (487–593): The twenty-ninth patriarch in line from the Buddha and the second Chinese patriarch, after Bodhidharma. His Chinese name is Hui-K'o. Before receiving the transmission of the Dharma from Bodhidharma, he was known as Jinko (Shen-kuang), or Divine Light, because prior to his birth a strange light filled his parents' room. For more on his life, see the chapter "Bodhidharma's *Outline of Practice.*"

Obaku Kiun (d. ca. 850): Rinzai's teacher, who received the transmission of the Dharma from Hyakujo Ekai (Pai-chang Huai-hai; 749–814). Obaku, known in Chinese as Huang-po Hsi-yuan, was a master of huge functioning. Far beyond any normal standards, he was truly honest and free from extraneous thinking. Constantly studying the sutras and the records of the ancients' lives or doing prostrations, with everything he did he realized the true life of a patriarch.

Patriarchs: On Vulture Peak, the Buddha said to Makakasho Sonja, "I have the True Dharma Eye, the Marvelous Mind of Nirvana, the True Form of the Formless, the Subtle Dharma Gate, which does not set up words and phrases, and is a separate transmission outside the scriptures. This I entrust to you Makakasho." In just this way, the Buddha Mind, as it is, was realized. From vessel to vessel this same state of mind was passed on through deep realization and correct understanding. Those who received this Buddha Mind and passed it on are called the patriarchs.

Rinzai Gigen (d. 867): The founder of the Rinzai sect and the disciple to whom Obaku's Dharma was transmitted, Rinzai was the twenty-eighth patriarch after Bodhidharma. Known in Chinese as Lin-chi I-Hsuan, Rinzai is said to have been sharp and strong in quality, like a general who is urging on great troops. In his *Rinzai-roku*, or *Records of Rinzai*, we can see clearly the meticulousness with which he taught, but also the freedom and expansiveness of his way. In this world, with people attached to profit and self-benefit and political power, we become completely unable to believe in each other. Rinzai Zenji knew this well and could guide people from this way of functioning to the truth.

Rohatsu osesshin: The most intense one-week sesshin of the year, in which people of training make one great determined effort to let go of all external matters. *Ro* is a Japanese word for December, and *hatsu* is the Japanese word for eighth. It was on the eighth of December that the Buddha is said to have seen the morning star shining and awakened to his True Nature. From ancient times this has been considered the sesshin in which one must lose one's life completely; only after doing this sesshin is one considered to be a true person of training. It is impossible to count how many have realized their True Nature through the opportunity of the Rohatsu osesshin.

Roshi: A Zen master.

Ryokan (1758–1831): Born in Echigo, in Nigata Prefecture, Ryokan trained at Entsuji in Okayama Prefecture, where he clarified the very marrow of Soto Zen. He then returned to Echigo and, because he remained unattached to any of formalities of Soto Zen, was able to live in such a way that his individual freedom was never lost. Not being moved around by society, he was a genuine example of an essence that is so hard to find in today's society, so centered is it on dualism, limited past experience, and

GLOSSARY

intellectual knowledge. For those who cannot let go of these concerns, he is a shining example and guide.

Samadhi: If someone wants to play the piano well, he or she needs to forget the fingers, forget the music, and forget the keys; forgetting all of that, a person can then become the music completely. This is samadhi. Likewise, people who play a sport, or people who are artists, have to let go of their own small-minded opinions and let the larger Mind move through them. While having and working with a material object, to be able to let go of all concepts, and to also let go of one's own smaller self so that one can function freely, is samadhi.

Samu: In a Zen dojo it is said, "First is samu, second is zazen, third is reading the sutras." Samu is physical work, but it is also zazen in action. Samu has a spiritual emphasis and is more than just physical work to the extent that through it you can give life to your Buddha Nature. When Dogen Zenji was in China he met an elderly *tenzo*, or cook, who was drying shiitake mushrooms in the extreme heat. This was such a torturous task that Dogen asked the tenzo why he hadn't asked one of the many younger monks to do the work for him. The elderly tenzo answered, "They are not me." It is easy to ask someone else to complete a task, but only you can use your own True Nature to fulfill your work. Here is samu's deepest meaning. When Obaku's teacher, Hyakujo Ekai, gave us the rules of the dojo, he said that all people should do samu equally. Even when he was very elderly, Kyakujo continued to work in the garden every day. His monks were so worried about him that they begged him not to work, and finally one of the young monks hid his tools. When Hyakujo found his tools gone he went into his room and would not come out even for meals. When asked if he was ill, he replied with the famous words, "A day of no work is a day of no food." Through samu, as long as we can move we can offer our lives to society. Samu is not conceptual work; it is an actualization of the essence of Zen.

Sangha: *Sangha* does not refer just to those who have shaved their heads and wear the robes of a monk. Those who are working to clarify the mind that unites all beings in harmony—and then function in society with that harmonious mind, forgetting their own small selves—are the true sangha. In society, we all are trying to advance our own opinions and get our own way. The true sangha is not a form or a way to be, it is to always put others first without emphasizing your own opinion. With this kind of mind we build a harmonious society. This way of being is called a sangha.

Sanzen: The process of encountering a true teacher so that one's ego attachments can be removed and the state of mind of the Buddha and the patriarchs can be realized. It is also called the great furnace or the great anvil. This is because, like any excellent cutting tool, one's Buddha Nature has to be forged over and over in a very hot flame and then pounded again and again to remove all the impurities. Sanzen is not a process of vague discussion or of analyzing one's personality. To get rid of the impurities in our mind we must work on it over and over until we finally realize directly our pure clear mind.

Satori: The Japanese term for the experience of enlightenment. The terms *kensho* and *satori* have almost exactly the same meaning and are often used interchangeably. See *Kensho*.

Sesshin: One week of continuous zazen with breaks only for sutras, eating, and sleeping. Sesshin allows one to spend seven days deepening one's inner being, gathering the mind in order to

GLOSSARY

encounter and touch True Mind. See the chapter "Sesshin."

Shakyamuni (567–433 B.C.): Literally, Shakyamuni means "the sage of the Shakyas." In the northeast area of India, in what is today Nepal, Shakyamuni was born as Gautama Siddhartha, the heir to the throne of the Shakya clan. Gautama Siddhartha threw away everything in order to understand life's deepest meaning, to know the source of pain and suffering, and to find the true joy for all in society. In the mountains he did six years of ascetic training, and finally at Bodhgaya, under the bodhi tree, he sat silently and encountered the radiance of the morning star, realizing humans' clear mind as it becomes one with the material world of form. From a two-dimensional dualistic perspective he entered a single-dimensional world beyond differentiation. From this experience he went to teach his friends in Deer Park, and until the age of eighty he worked continuously to liberate people. The historical person who actually lived twenty-five hundred years ago was the first to realize this truth and how to teach it, and this same truth has been passed down to us by the patriarchs and continues to liberate people today.

Sixth patriarch (638–713): The sixth successor in the Dharma after Bodhidharma, known in Japan as Rokuso Eno and in China as Hui-neng, became enlightened in his youth upon hearing a passage from the *Diamond Sutra*.

Susokkan: When we are born, we are naturally in samadhi with our breathing, and from the time of our birth until our death we are never apart from our breathing. In accordance with this samadhi of breathing, by doing susokkan we focus on our life energy exactly as it is—letting go of our attachments to knowledge, past experiences, and other decorations that obscure our essence. We do not just watch our breath, however, but rather exhale completely and let go of extraneous thoughts and deepen to the point where we know the state of mind beyond separation into outside and inside. We go to where our breath is that of the whole universe and we become one with all of life. This is the true essence of susokkan, which is explained in more detail in the chapter "Zazen."

Sutra: From ancient times we have the three-part division of sutras, precepts, and doctrine. The precepts are about how we live in accordance with the essence of awareness. The doctrine is the essence of enlightenment as expressed in words. Sutras are the enlightenment of the Buddha as it is. The sutras cannot be interpreted, nor can anything be added to or taken away from them. If there is any interpretation at all it is a big mistake. When translated, sutras become doctrine; thus, only those written in Sanskrit are beyond interpretation and the real thing. A sutra is the essence of the Buddha's enlightenment, not words about it.

Takuhatsu: The traditional Buddhist alms rounds, sometimes called "begging" in English. It is said that one cannot do takuhatsu with a proud mind; one must become humble. To be able to receive and give with an empty mind, with no ego attachment rising, is the point of the practice of takuhatsu.

Tanden: The point in the body considered by Eastern medicine to be the physiological, psychic, and spiritual center of the body. In Japanese, *tan* means elixir, that is, life energy; *den* means rice field or to raise abundantly. With the tanden we abundantly give rise to life energy. From our tanden we vibrantly bring forth ki that can affect even the atmosphere around us, and we can then offer this energy of revitalization to many people. For more on the tanden, see the chapter "Zazen."

GLOSSARY

Transmission of the Lamp: Among the earliest surviving histories of Zen Buddhism, the *Transmission of the Lamp* was compiled in 1004 by Tao-yuan.

Yamada Mumon (1900–1988): One of the foremost men of the Rinzai sect, Yamada Mumon was known for his high level of activity and functioning. When he was young, his father wanted him to become a lawyer. While in law school, he heard that Confucius had said that, rather than presiding over trials, the true goal was to make a world where there is no need for trials. Upon hearing this, Mumon Roshi began to search for a way to make a world where there is no need for lawyers. One day he heard that Kawaguchi Ekai had returned from China and went to hear him speak. Kawaguchi taught that if we could cover the entire world in soft leather, then we could walk everywhere without ever cutting our feet. But since that is not possible, what we can do instead is put soft leather on the bottoms of our own feet, so that everywhere we walk is soft. Likewise, while it is impossible to put a roof over the entire world, if everyone had an umbrella we could all walk anywhere protected from the rain. To save every single person seems to be impossible, but if one person's mind clearly experiences and expresses the truth, then many people will find the soft shoes and umbrella of awakening. This is the way of the Bodhisattva. Even if one person cannot literally liberate all people, each person who realizes the truth will manifest true light and show the possibility of awakening to all people without ceasing. Mumon Roshi became a student of Kawaguchi Ekai, but in attempting to follow this path with his own body he became very ill with tuberculosis. After living in isolation for several years, on one clear bright June day he saw a nanten flower and wrote this poem:

THE PATH TO BODHIDHARMA

All things are embraced
Within the universal mind
Told by the cool wind
This morning.

He was deeply awakened and with this his body was cured. He went to a sesshin at Empukuji near Kyoto and was able to completely realize his True Nature. He then went to Tenryuji, and under Seisetsu Genjo deepened his state of mind until, at the age of fifty-one, he became a master. He went first to teach at Kyoto's Reiunin Temple, and then became the master of Shofukuji Temple in Kobe, where he raised many disciples. During the Second World War, while with Seisetsu Roshi, he visited many places of war, and what he saw left him with deep feelings of repentance. In 1967, he went on pilgrimages to various Southeast Asian countries to apologize to and say sutras for the war dead of all religions. By doing this he repented the horrible war, and he taught this posture of repentance to his students as well. Although he knew only a few words of English, he taught many students from abroad and made many strong karmic connections. He traveled to the opening of Dai Bosatsu Zendo in New York State, to the San Francisco Zen Center, to the Mount Baldy Zen Center in California, and to Mexico. He made a pilgrimage to India and at Bodhgaya built a Japanese temple. He went to Europe and opened the East West Spiritual Exchange between Catholicism and Buddhism, himself entering and living in nine contemplative monasteries in Europe, experiencing the life of the monks there. His disciples settled all over Europe, strengthening his extensive karmic ties with the West. He later went on to become the abbot of Myoshinji and the head of Hanazono College. He was a brilliant scholar and a great master with many disciples, but he never accepted any words of praise; instead, he lived his entire life as just one citizen. This was Yamada Mumon Roshi.

GLOSSARY

Yoka Gengaku (665–713): The Zen master known primarily for the work attributed to him entitled *Shodoka*, often translated as *Song of Enlightenment*. His Chinese name is Yen-chia Hsuan-chueh.

Zazen: Meditation; sitting in which one cuts all connections with the external world and lets go of all concerns within. See the chapter "Zazen."

Zendo: The meditation hall in which monks live and people practice zazen.

Zenji: An ordained man.